More praise for Faye Knol's Receivin

"If you have ever wondered what love looks like, this book is a good place to begin to find out. . . . David brought new understanding of the meaning of love to his family; his story will challenge, unsettle, and inspire readers to see the world differently — and perhaps see the providential significance of human disability. . . An excellent book. Very powerful."

> — **John Swinton** author of *Raging with Compassion:*
> *Pastoral Responses to the Problem of Evil*

"Goodness, what a story! What a beautiful, true writer Faye Knol is. This hazelnut of a book is honest, not sugarcoated. Knol conveys the daily tensions as well as the glimmering miracles that land in this family. Her prose is crystal clear, like carefully cut glass. Perhaps most striking in her story, and most compelling, is the crucial, continued support of friends, grandparents, fellow church members, and neighbors. David's life was a blessing and also a work of love for a team. Read this book in a group, and pray for such work to come your way."

> — **Amy Laura Hall** author of *Conceiving Parenthood:*
> *American Protestantism and the Spirit of Reproduction*

"Now you have the opportunity to receive David too — and he will change your life, if you let him, by all he will teach you. Bless God for the depth of spiritual Joy the Knol family is passing on through this book! Thank God for the myriads of beautiful gifts that David's affectionate spirit and intimate friendships offer to us still!"

— **Marva Dawn** author of *Being Well When We Are Ill* and *Joy in Our Weakness*

"Faye Knol writes with incredible honesty, love, and clarity, vividly describing David in all his uniqueness. David's road to heaven as experienced through his family's eyes is something not to be missed. . . . He was a model of God's grace to all of us."

— **Nella Uitvlugt** executive director of Friendship Ministries

receiving david

the gift of a son who taught us
how to live and love

faye knol

William B. Eerdmans Publishing Company
Grand Rapids, Michigan / Cambridge, U.K.

Published 2010 by

Wm. B. Eerdmans Publishing Co.

2140 Oak Industrial Drive N.E., Grand Rapids, Michigan 49505 /

P.O. Box 163, Cambridge CB3 9PU U.K.

Printed in the United States of America

16 15 14 13 12 11 10   7 6 5 4 3 2 1

Library of Congress Cataloging-in-Publication Data

Knol, Faye, 1957–

    Receiving David / Faye Knol

        p.   cm.

ISBN 978-0-8028-6543-4 (pbk. : alk. paper)

1. Knol, Faye, 1957–   2. Knol, David Harry, 1982–2005.   3. Parents
of children with disabilities — Biography.   4. Parents of children with
disabilities — Psychology.   5. Children with mental disabilities — Family
relationships.   I. Title.

    HQ759.913.K57 2010

    155.9′37092 — dc22

    [B]

                                                            2010022495

www.eerdmans.com

contents

preface

Life took a wildly unexpected turn the day my second child was born. He arrived dangerously early and was not expected to survive, let alone live a life of independence and opportunity. Yet he came to achieve a measure of both and over the course of his twenty-two years worked himself securely into our hearts and souls.

His family grew to need him as much as he needed us.

David taught us how to live and love. He showed us the joy that comes from living in relationship with others. And he invited us to view the world in a new and better way. Yet we didn't see this possibility when we first met him in 1982. Not even remotely.

Throughout his life, David's brother, sister, father, and I worked as a team to provide the care he required. Faithful friends and family displayed God's grace to us. Outstanding educators encouraged and worked with him to help him reach a remarkable level of confidence and independence. Exceptional medical professionals guided us along the way and walked right beside us as we entered the valley of the shadow of death.

Losing David was crushing, and the pain remains deep. But we retain his spirit and joy in the lives we live today. He taught us how to live and then he helped us learn that death need not be feared.

acknowledgments

Thank you to the many people who believed in the value of sharing this story. My special thanks to those who read through early drafts and provided early encouragement, feedback, perspective, and never-ending enthusiasm.

Deepest gratitude is given to Eve Clayton for editing the original manuscript. Her insight and respect for the story bolstered my strength and spirit, enabling me to proceed.

I am grateful to Nick Wolterstorff for reviewing the manuscript and recommending it to the Eerdmans Publishing Company. What a lovely moment it was for our family when we learned of the book's acceptance from Jon Pott, who became my editor. Jon's careful work ensured that David's life was captured thoughtfully; his guidance assured me that David's story was safe in his hands. Tracey Gebbia, the book's designer, truly grasped David's personality as she lent her expertise to the design, layout, and photo selection. And my thanks to Jeff Dykehouse, some of whose wonderful photographs of David and our family grace this book.

I am immensely thankful for each person who was involved.

Still, there would be no story to tell had it not been for David, Harry, Jared, and Rachel. We lived and grew together.

"We give back to you, O God, those whom you gave to us. You did not lose them when you gave them to us, and we do not lose them by their return to you."

William Penn (1644–1718)

receiving david

For privacy, the names of the doctors and nurses mentioned in this story have been changed.

a precarious beginning

What is going on here?

Our son David was born on December 14, 1982. He arrived fourteen weeks premature and we were told that he was not expected to live more than a few hours. His vital signs were weak; his eyes were still fused shut. He weighed only one pound, fourteen ounces. So he was simply handed to us, wrapped securely in a soft blanket. It was half past four in the morning.

Filled with love and sorrow, my husband Harry and I gently cradled this tiny boy, our second child. We had been debating names, and as we gazed at him, the name David seemed to fit. Unsettled and unsure of what was going on, we watched his shallow, weak breaths and held him close. He was so tiny, his head no larger than a tennis ball.

A week earlier, I had undergone tests indicating a complication of pregnancy called partial placenta previa. No need for great alarm, I was told, just don't vacuum or lift anything heavy. It was the Christmas season — we had a calendar full of planned events.

Within hours of learning this news, I began premature labor. Harry was away at a meeting the evening of December 7. What I first tried to ignore became an issue to present to him when he walked in the door later that night. A phone call to the doctor

directed us to head right to the hospital. The next
seven days and nights were spent at the hospital,
mostly in the labor room, where I was given strong
medications in an attempt to stop the premature labor.
But my labor pains prevailed. The medical team gave
us little hope for delivering a child who could survive;
they tried to prepare us. Mid-December — and our
baby was not due until late March — this could not be
good.

After his birth, the delivery room nurse checked
on us frequently, kindly asking if she should take him.
Take him? Take him where? To the newborn nursery,
she said, where he might be warmer. Until he dies?
I wondered, while Harry thought, until he warms
up? It was years before the two of us realized we had
conflicting interpretations of that moment.

Time passed, and my nurse, Linda, eventually
carried our baby away from us down a brightly lit
hallway and watched as his eyes inexplicably fluttered
and then opened. In the newborn nursery, Linda
noticed his breathing and color improving, as David
fought to live.

Meanwhile, wanting to share the news of David's
arrival, Harry and I telephoned our parents and pastor.
David's outlook was grim, we said. While we had
hoped that he would be strong enough to live, all hope
was swept away with the doctors' belief that it was not
to be so. We wept, exhausted and filled with sadness.

Accompanying our sorrow was a sense of regret that, for fear of disturbing him, neither of us had opened the blanket to look at his fingers and toes.

More time passed. Sensing he was stronger than the doctors had believed, Linda called her nursing supervisor. A doctor was called to reassess our baby, and soon one of the staff, bypassing the elevator, raced David up the stairs to the Neonatal Intensive Care Unit (NICU) to seek more help.

Then, shortly, several hospital staff — Linda, the OB doctor, a NICU nurse, and the NICU resident — came to my room to tell Harry and me that David had been rushed to the NICU. They showed us Polaroid pictures taken minutes earlier of David, his eyes wide open. Did we want to see him?

Of course. So they wheeled my bed into the elevator and took us up to the strange, amazing world of the NICU.

Now, as a nurse positioned me next to David's treatment table in the triage room, I looked at him with wonder. He was pink and lying with his eyes open under a hood of oxygen. Seeing him again and hearing he was doing better than expected, I was overjoyed.

Harry, on the other hand, slumped against a wall, horrified. *What is going on here? What has been done?* Our son's color had been gray and his breathing irregular for quite some time. A special education teacher, Harry recognized the gravity of the situation, understood the damage that can result when oxygen and other assistance are withheld. One of the staff found a chair for him to sit on as he buried his head in his hands.

Long months in the hospital

Given David's fragile condition, it was six weeks before we were able to hold him again. We visited the hospital every day, often twice a day, to caress and talk to him. Struggling to grasp what was happening from day to day, we wrestled with the uncertainty of David's life. Minute by minute things would change. Hopes rose and were dashed. Living hour by hour, we gradually built an emotional armor around ourselves, a shield from fear and grief.

David's stay in the NICU lasted nearly five months, during which time he endured thirteen surgical procedures. He also suffered through infections, liver and intestinal failure, kidney failure, broken bones, unknown neurological damage, and eye damage resulting in blindness. Many nights we did not know whether he would live to the next morning.

In the NICU we became acquainted with several other families who had premature infants. Each baby took his or her own route through the ordeal of prematurity. Witnessing the differences in our various experiences, we were gradually able to understand why the doctors could not give us the concrete predictions we so wanted.

Home, finally

On May 6, 1983, we took David home from the hospital.

Harry and I had been married nearly six years. My first pregnancy had been uneventful, with Jared arriving just a few weeks early, robust and resilient. Jared, who had just turned two, was young enough to enjoy the attention family members and friends provided him while we spent so much time at the hospital with David.

Eager to finally take David home from the hospital, Harry and I were also apprehensive when the responsibility of his demanding care fell to us.

Weeks before David's birth, at a family Thanksgiving gathering, one of Harry's cousins came up to me before leaving and said, "I hope that your pregnancy and delivery go well, Faye." At the time I thought his concern was kind but unnecessary — I was doing fine. But remembering his words later, I realized that no pregnancy could ever be assumed to be routine.

There was much we needed to learn.

home life: the first two years

At home we were presented with new challenges. Since David wasn't strong enough to drink from a bottle, we had learned in the hospital how to place a feeding tube into his nose, leading to his stomach, allowing him to be fed directly.

Along with David's feedings, multiple medications, oxygen use, monitors, and overall fragility, we had the ongoing care of Jared. An energetic delight to us, Jared kept us from being consumed with David's care. We were glad for the distraction he provided.

Though uncertain and often overwhelmed, we did the best we could and learned whatever was necessary to meet David's many needs.

Resuming life

Harry, bringing a special education teacher's perspective, resolved that David should be treated as a part of the family, not the center of it. We should try to live as normal a life as possible. Naturally more cautious, I had a hard time seeing how that could happen, but Harry was serious Within weeks of David's homecoming, Harry decided we should ask our twelve-year-old neighbor Jill — the oldest of four and a responsible girl — to come over and watch Jared and David so we could go out. "I don't think so! ' I said. My good, persistent husband insisted that we needed to get out and that David would be fine if we were gone for only an hour.

"I am going to go," Harry gently insisted, "and I hope you will come with me. We can't let this baby make us feel trapped. We need to find ways to refresh ourselves, even if for only an hour or two." After thinking a few more minutes, I agreed. We called Jill, who was willing to come over (with her very competent mother at home next door), and we left David and Jared in her care for a little over an hour.

Also, soon after David came home, a casual acquaintance began inviting Harry to join him fly-fishing. Not having seen Harry interested in fishing before, I was surprised at how readily he accepted the invitation. Quickly, fly-fishing became a much-loved hobby to pursue with this new friend. Harry encouraged me to find time myself to leave the demands of home while he would care for our sons. I began to nurture my friendships with other women and planned activities, events, and getaways. So, while we did find things we could enjoy together, we also valued discovering separate ways of re-energizing ourselves.

Over the years I realized that these were critical points in our life with David. While watching who David would become, we were determined not to lose our individual selves.

Early therapy

In September 1983, David, now nine months old, began receiving twice-weekly services through the local public school special education diagnostic center. A teacher with visual impairment certification came to our home one morning a week to work with David and me. Anne quickly became a wonderful resource, offering gentle, loving support and direction. She even brought games and books for Jared to enjoy, making him part of the process.

David also received therapy at school one morning a week, and I was required to attend a weekly parent support-group meeting at the same time. This did not appeal to me, so I tried to get out of it, thinking it would be an ideal time to get groceries. "How about I just drop David off for his therapy and pick him up at the end of the session?" I suggested. But the rules were firm: David would not receive assistance if I didn't attend the parent group. So, grudgingly, I consented, not pleased to be sitting in a room full of other parents of children with disabilities and challenges. *No time for this*, I grumbled.

A psychologist led the group, teaching us about disabilities and providing opportunities for us to share our questions and concerns. How did we feel about the delay or disability our child had? How did I *feel* about it? Up to that point I hadn't allowed myself to think much about that question — no energy. I had been raised to press on and deal with life; feelings just weren't a high priority.

For well over a year, as David went to therapy, I attended the parent meeting. Gradually it became a welcome, safe place for me. The psychologist slowly wore down my defenses and led me to recognize, acknowledge, and then verbalize the grief and fears I had about David and his future.

I have always looked back at that fragile period as the time I began learning how to deal with David — to grieve the losses he experienced and to generate the strength to move forward.

Medical issues

We had been warned to watch for bowel obstructions, the result of scarring from David's repeated colon blockages and surgeries in the NICU. Instead, we faced two episodes of aspiration pneumonia that required hospitalization during his first year home. During the second bout, in January 1984, we became aware that he had also developed a specific seizure pattern. This condition caused David to lose all responsiveness and forced us to return to tube feedings after five months of bottle-feeding.

When the seizures first developed, Harry and I were already exhausted from David's ongoing care. Now multiple tests would be necessary to assess the seizure pattern. Seeing that I was not emotionally capable of facing yet another ordeal, Harry rearranged his work schedule so he could take David for the testing. This was a lovely gesture toward our marriage, cementing the fact that we were in this together and would support each other throughout. We realized each other's need to balance the care load in order to go on day after day.

While David was in the hospital for treatment of these seizures, we received training in how to administer injections of a medication intended to stimulate brain activity. Once he came home, we continued the injections, but for months David only slept, responding very little. Devastated, we were told that we faced three possible outcomes — David would die soon, remain unresponsive, or respond to the medication, though with possible new damage to the brain.

Gradually he did begin to respond. Over time he again learned to drink from a bottle. Later we introduced pureed food by spoon — but for years David would not chew. Waiting for him to swallow was enormously frustrating, so Harry and I developed a system: We'd put a spoonful of food in David's mouth and then step away, glancing periodically to see whether he had swallowed. It was often five, ten, fifteen minutes, or more, between each bite.

Eventually David grew stronger — but it was wearing on the rest of us. Patience is a virtue neither Harry or I had been naturally blessed with.

Legal questions

After David's first birthday we decided to seek legal advice on the circumstances surrounding his birth. The inevitable questions kept coming up. What could have been done differently at the time of David's birth? Was there mismanagement or negligence? The long period when he was breathing irregularly without assistance deprived him of oxygen, affecting several vital organs. A thorough investigation revealed that we did have legal avenues to pursue. Yet our attorney warned us that if we were to proceed, this could become a very public matter. Were we prepared for that?

After careful, prayerful consideration of the legal — and human — questions, Harry and I decided that this was the child we had prayed for and asked for; who were we to question the child we had been given, and under what circumstances? A peace enveloped both of us. We decided to put the legal process to rest and proceed with life as it evolved.

David's eye trouble

During his stay in the NICU, David's eyes had been checked periodically. We knew that eye damage could occur in premature infants, but since his initial eye checks looked okay and he was facing so many episodes that were life threatening, we did not devote much energy to this concern. That changed one Saturday morning in April 1983, about a month before we brought David home from the hospital.

Harry was at work and I was home with Jared. The telephone rang. It was an ophthalmologist, who had just checked David's eyes. Concerns he had noted earlier had developed into serious problems, he said. David's vision would be greatly impaired owing to a condition called retrolental fibroplasia. (Years later it became known as retinopathy of prematurity.) He told me about an ophthalmologist on the other side of the state who was having limited success reattaching the retinas of extremely premature infants.

Distraught and apprehensive, I questioned him extensively. After hanging up, I paced around the house, overwhelmed and frightened by this new complication, one more concern added to the many we already had about David's health and future.

Minutes later the phone rang again. I thought about not answering it, but then did. It was my friend Flori calling from her home in California to see how I was doing. *How was I doing?* Deciding I couldn't share the news I had just received — it was more than I could handle — I talked in general of how David was faring in the NICU. The love, concern, and compassion she provided from miles away calmed me down.

Feeling comforted by a longtime friend, I paused to wonder at the timing of her call. Perhaps we were not meandering aimlessly, even though things seemed out of control.

The ophthalmologist said David's eyes should be further assessed as soon as possible. So after David had recovered somewhat from his latest intestinal surgery, we arranged to drive him across the state for a consultation and possible surgery. We loaded David into the car with his feeding tubes, monitors, medications, and everything we would need for a few days' stay. A NICU nurse accompanied us on the 150-mile trip.

The ophthalmologist there agreed that David needed surgery but would not operate because, he said, David had a slight fever. We returned to the NICU the same day, frustrated and disappointed. More frustration followed when we returned for eye surgery a month later and learned that David's eyes had greatly deteriorated since our April visit.

Still, we decided to return there and go ahead with several eye surgeries, once David had been discharged from the NICU, to see if his retinas could be reattached.

After the first surgery, while David was in the pediatric intensive care unit, Harry and I slipped down to the hospital cafeteria for lunch. Across the large, crowded room I recognized a woman in hospital scrubs as someone I had known in college. Lacking the energy to explain why we were there, I let the opportunity to speak to her pass by.

Later that afternoon I stepped away from David's side and left the ICU. Walking down a hallway, I saw this same woman standing alone right in front of me, waiting for an elevator. *Maybe I am meant to connect with her,* I thought.

I introduced myself, and she remembered me. Once I explained our situation, she asked where we were staying during David's recovery and insisted that we stay in her home, just blocks from the hospital. She and her husband had a guest bedroom. If we chose to stay, she said, they would simply give us a key so we could come and go as we pleased.

That night at the hotel, Harry and I discussed her offer, not really feeling up to interacting with people we did not know well. But she looked us up the next day in the pediatric ICU and told us that her husband, whom we had never met, also extended the invitation. So we accepted the offer and were overwhelmed with their generosity and their respect for our fragile state of mind. We ended up staying with this couple during each of David's future eye surgeries over the next year and a half and will never forget their gracious hospitality.

When David was two, we faced a crossroads. Despite several experimental eye surgeries, his vision had not been restored.

Decision time came when I was in the hospital after having delivered our daughter Rachel. I encouraged Harry to keep a scheduled appointment with the ophthalmologist the day after Rachel's birth. The eye specialist suggested more surgery for David, and we had to decide whether to continue. We recalled how after each surgery David had to be kept upright to reduce pressure on the eyes. In fact, he had been kept in upright positions for most of his life at home with us.

Harry and I discussed and agreed, as we held our new daughter, that it was time to stop the experimental eye surgeries. We were satisfied to have tried them, but realized it was time to work on other areas of David's life.

For years, if asked, I replied that David was visually impaired. I couldn't bear to say the word *blind*. It sounded so final and harsh. Gradually, over time, it became okay.

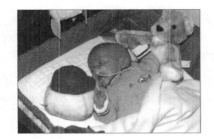

david at age two: intensely needy

Choosing a pediatrician

Before David's second birthday, Dr. Thomas had become David's pediatrician. I spent a great deal of time with Dr. Thomas on our first visit, carefully reviewing the details of David's birth and the traumas he had experienced in the months thereafter. I felt the need to fully explain David and our view of the circumstances surrounding his birth before we could establish a trusting relationship.

Dr. Thomas recalled the stories he had heard from fellow physicians about our son in the NICU. Hospital protocol had been followed, he explained, when David was handed to us right after birth. But, he went on to say, several hospital protocols were changed from then on because of David's experience.

Dr. Thomas became a vital part of David's life and care, always greeting him with enthusiasm and being attentive to our concerns and stress. We grew together, as he offered encouragement and praise for the care we provided David. And because he knew David's precarious beginning, he also marveled at the strides David later made. Balancing realism, joy, and concern, Dr. Thomas walked with us throughout David's life.

Prayer and change

Harry began a daily routine of praying for David to become happy. I will admit I found this irritating. We had prayed for big things in David's brief life, and many of the answers we had hoped for had not developed. I thought Harry's idea was a waste of time, and too simple.

In David's first year, many well-meaning people had sent us poems about "special children," and we often heard comments about others' not being able to handle a child such as David. These clichés weren't necessarily helpful and often fell flat.

Yet, we were learning to see God's presence and help in ways we had not expected. Knowing that prayers for strength were offered on our behalf, we became aware of a gradual change in our hearts toward life. Because caring for David was so time-consuming, we could no longer do things spontaneously; however, we began to find other, surprising opportunities for pleasure and fun. New people entered our life, and help came from unexpected places. We did not feel abandoned, but drew support in a variety of ways from the people around us.

The support of friends

Once David and I began the weekly program at the diagnostic center, arranging care for Jared during these sessions took a great deal of energy. Soon, however, someone became aware of this need and volunteered to watch Jared each Tuesday morning. Not knowing Diane very well, I was surprised but grateful for her eager commitment.

The parent sessions were often so intense that I would return to Diane's house with a headache and frayed emotions. She provided a listening ear and a cup of tea every week when David and I came to collect Jared. Over the years she found many ways to help and love David; her free spirit and generous nature would bless us all of David's life.

At the same time, we were aware that many of our peers did not grasp the extra strength and effort it took for us to care for David. Hearing the distress friends would have over their child's ear infection did not sit well with me, and I would have to remind myself to be sensitive to their needs. However, others who were older and had finished raising their children shared with us their understanding of the endless care and unknown future we had with David. We deeply appreciated their empathy, insight, and encouragement.

The school bus

In January 1985 David, at two years old, was strong enough to begin half-day school programming five days a week. We were eager for him to receive all the therapy and stimulation he could but had a hard time imagining him on a school bus. I could have driven him back and forth each day, but I also had at the same time to provide transportation for Jared, who by then was in preschool.

I decided to give the bus a try. The first day was cold and snowy. I had Jared and David ready, and my car set to go. When the bus arrived, I walked down the driveway, six months pregnant, with thirteen-pound David in one arm and his car seat in the other. After meeting the driver and settling David into his seat, I rushed to my car with Jared, and we followed the bus to school. The staff had assured me that David would be well cared for, but I needed the reassurance of seeing the process unfold.

Jared and I watched the staff unload David from the bus and carry him into school. We then returned home, satisfied to have witnessed everything run smoothly. Probably to the staff's relief, I never felt the need to follow again, and David always enjoyed his bus rides. That he was picked up and dropped off right at our driveway was a convenience we always appreciated. Over the years he had wonderful bus drivers who lovingly cared for him.

Getting David ready for the school day was a long, slow process, and Harry and I began a system, because neither of us wanted sole responsibility. My job was to get David up and dressed and prepare food for him. Then Harry would take over, feeding David and placing him on the bus. This routine was rarely broken.

Welcoming Rachel

As a participant in weekly parent support groups while David received therapy, I learned of countless complications that could prevent a healthy birth. When our daughter, Rachel, arrived five weeks early in March 1985, the NICU team was present at her delivery, along with Linda, the same delivery nurse who had assisted at David's birth. She told us that upon arriving at work that morning she had barely stepped off the elevator when co-workers met her and announced that I was delivering, so she came straight over.

Rachel Anne — true to the passionate, spirited person she is to this day — arrived at 8:00 a.m., crying loudly and her eyes wide open. She was small, but in fine form. What a cause for celebration. We had wanted another child and, not knowing what David's progress would be, had hoped for one sooner rather than later. David's care, we had reasoned, would likely remain a constant no matter how long we waited. In the meantime, Jared was growing older. With thankfulness to God, we joyfully received Rachel and reveled in the miracle of her healthy birth.

ages three through six: ups and downs

David's developmental process continued to bring disappointments. He was often miserable and would arch his back in response to our touch. With all the surgeries, injections, and tube feedings he had endured, human touch had become a frightful experience in his dark, confusing world.

The disappointment was so painful that we began deliberately not hoping for anything concerning David's future. We decided to be surprised by *any* progress he made but to expect nothing as we continued to do all we could to love and care for him. Our focus was simply on living. Harry's teaching schedule at that time conveniently allowed him to return home at a reasonable time, so our duties were shared, something we both insisted on.

A slow transformation

Over the years — and I do emphasize *years* — a slow transformation began to take place in David. Sometime after his second birthday, he began to sit up on his own, a tremendous accomplishment that thrilled us all — not least David himself!

Then, around the age of four, he began his first recognizable verbal communication: He hummed a song often sung in his preschool class. Over time, he began humming other familiar songs. This led to his using single words, which slowly expanded as he learned to put more words together.

When David approached his fifth birthday, we decided to hold an open-house birthday party, inviting everyone who had supported him and all of us. We were amazed to have reached this point, with David becoming reasonably stable and healthy and Harry and me surviving many adjustments and challenges.

Although we did not say so to others, Harry and I decided it was also a party for us.

A look ahead

When David was five, Harry identified three things that would make David happier (and our care for him easier): continence, the ability to walk, and the ability to communicate his basic needs. Great ideas, however unlikely they seemed to pull off. How differently we were now coming to view what was important in life.

Though I tried not to think too far into the future, I did sometimes wonder how I'd be able to handle David physically as he got older. So I began lifting weights to build my upper-body strength. I knew this would be good for me anyway, plus I wanted to be able to manage and care for David always.

When David was older and larger, friends sometimes wondered whether I could still physically handle him. Good question — by the time he reached his growth potential, he was very strong and only slightly smaller than my five-foot-one-inch frame. Still, I was usually able to intervene or lead him away when a problem arose. It may not have been a pretty sight, but David usually responded quickly.

ages seven through nine:
astonishing developments

At seven, David began full-day school programming in the local public school system. His educational label was "severely multiply impaired" — quite a mouthful — but Harry had helped me early on to not be disturbed by any label David would be given, saying, "A label will not change who David is and what he may accomplish."

This label encompassed his visual impairments, his cognitive delays, and his small stature. It also allowed him to receive summer-school programming, which thrilled us. We wanted David to receive as much stimulation as possible. We were thankful to be living in Michigan, where special education is available through age twenty-six.

Often we were asked what school was like for David. Not many people in our circle had seen a center-based school program for children with special needs. David's class typically had around eight children, and three staff members, and the instruction emphasized skills for daily living. Along with eating skills, sensory stimulation, and appropriate social skills, students were introduced to a variety of ideas and activities and went on many community outings.

Everything in the classroom that belonged to David was identified with a piece of sandpaper: his place at the table, his coat hook, his toothbrush, and whatever else. Other children had different tactile identifiers. David also received therapy from specialists, such as a mobility instructor, who helped him with maneuvering techniques.

At school the staff began taking David to the swimming pool. He hated it at first, just as he disliked taking baths. But gradually, as he adapted to the water in the school pool, he also began to enjoy baths at home.

The makings of happiness

The year he turned seven was an amazing year for David. He began walking. One day he simply stood up in our kitchen and took a few steps on his own, walking straight as could be! It was incredible! At seven he also began chewing food. This came after years of gradually adding texture to his food, with occasional guidance from a therapist at a nearby rehabilitation feeding clinic.

In another huge milestone that year, David became continent during the day. For months, Harry had been leading David to the bathroom and placing him on the toilet. Harry would then sit on the counter reading a book, waiting. Gradually David began having success, and with Harry's reinforcement, he achieved a new skill.

I waited until the process was routine before becoming involved, not sure I wanted to waste my energy on this new goal of Harry's until I saw some progress. One day as David was sitting on the toilet and I was waiting, he suddenly began to sing, "God is so good, God is so good, God is so good, He's so good to me." David listened to a wide variety of music, but it amazed me to hear those words coming out of his mouth. Then it dawned on me that while my son could sing such a song, I still looked at him through the lens of his limitations.

We had often felt that David's life should have been different. Now, little by little, we were beginning to see that David was exactly who he was always intended to be.

As David began to emerge and blossom, he became comfortable in his world. He began communicating his needs and developed an intense curiosity about the world around him. He welcomed meeting people and wanted to get to know anyone he met.

He also became comfortable with touch. In fact, touch gradually became vital to David as a source of security, love, and curiosity. He began to thrive on all types of touch and interaction. Predictably, he was resistant to every new experience he encountered, but we kept at it and found that with most things he gradually adapted.

What seemed to me too simple a development — David's becoming happy — turned out to make a tremendous difference in his world and our life. We were thankful beyond words and fully aware that this transformation was indeed remarkable.

Sibling relationships

Like any brother, David found ways to agitate his brother and sister — Rachel in particular. What amazed us was that instead of becoming distant and resentful toward him, she developed strategies, at a very young age, to stay one step ahead of him and find things he liked doing with her.

Rachel began many holiday traditions with David. She had him help her color Easter eggs, would write out his Valentines, and waved sparklers with him on the 4th of July. David came to love holidays! Their predictable routines gave him great pleasure. On Halloween he was a Friendly Ghost for years, visiting a couple of neighbors. Then he would sit near our front door, bouncing on the sofa with pleasure every time the doorbell rang and "Trick or Treat" was yelled.

When Jared and Rachel were young, they did not recognize David's disabilities. David was David. We were fascinated that other young children, often by age two, would stare at David, already aware of his uniqueness. We had several experiences with young children visiting our home, who, upon seeing David, would announce, "He *does* see — look, his eyes are open!" We always enjoyed helping children understand David and become comfortable around him.

One evening when Jared was in the fourth grade, David, then eight, accompanied us to Jared's school band concert. David liked music, so we were quite sure he would enjoy the concert. What we didn't anticipate was how hilarious David would find the young musicians' squeaks and squawks. With parents all around us proudly videotaping the event, David squealed with delight at every squeak he heard. This amused Harry and me, but since David was becoming a distraction, Harry took him out and missed most of the concert.

After that episode, Harry and I discussed most of Jared's and Rachel's events as they came up. If there was a chance that one of us would miss part of an important performance or game because of David, we would find someone to take care of him. We did not want Rachel or Jared to resent David for causing us to miss their events.

What unexpectedly worked in our favor was that David did not mind staying home with whoever came to care for him. He was usually delighted to have the chance to stay and interact with one of his regular caregivers. But he always wanted to know exactly where the rest of us were going and when we would be back. Being able to get away and knowing that David was well cared for and happy during events that weren't suited to him made *everyone* happy. Having opportunities to be spontaneous and devoted to Jared and Rachel exclusively, without all the extra attention David required, bolstered each one of us.

Jared and Rachel each spent much time caring for David as they grew older. Harry and I watched as a loving, natural feeling of responsibility towards David developed; they instinctively recognized his dependence on them, beginning when they were very young. In many ways David had four parents. We tried not to take advantage of Rachel and Jared but, unfortunately, sometimes we did. If they had an event they'd rather be at when we needed a caregiver, we would do everything possible to find a replacement.

Sometimes, however, they used David as a good excuse to get out of something — *sorry, I need to take care of my brother David.*

Caregivers

Our church family grew with David and loved him. Each Sunday, David accompanied us to church, where he spent time with faithful childcare attendants while we went to worship. Our friends' children were also comfortable with him, so it was easy to arrange for caregivers when we needed to go out for an evening. We enjoyed getting to know many young men and women who provided assistance.

Harry's parents, living nearby, willingly became our greatest help with David. They learned to manage all aspects of David's care, allowing us on occasion to take extended trips with the other children and make visits to my own parents and family who lived in California. We took David to California a few times, but as he became older, change in routine and environment made him more anxious and frustrated. Still, there were successes. When David was ten and the rest of us took a trip out West, Harry's parents tried having David sit through Sunday worship services with them. We weren't sure what to think of that when we returned home, but we continued what they had begun and it became our new routine. Amazingly, David adapted quickly to the predictable rhythm of worship services.

My parents came to Michigan several weeks every year to provide additional support and care. David adored all of his grandparents and was always ready to spend time with them. Their active involvement with David was the biggest factor in our ability to lead a full life.

ages ten through fifteen:
a personality in bloom

Growing independence

When David turned ten, it no longer seemed right to have him sleep in a crib. True, he remained very small, and he fit in the crib just fine; plus, he liked it, was safe, and never tried to climb out. Yet, now that he was ten, we decided to try him in a bed and see what would happen. I worried that David would either fall out or get up and wander around the house during the night. I imagined I'd get up in the morning and find him sleeping on the floor somewhere. But all my worrying was for nothing. David stayed in bed from the first night on, with a guardrail and a wall helping him identify his boundaries.

David continued his pattern of nighttime incontinence but increasingly would wake up, crying out during the night. When this happened, one of us would get him up and put him on the toilet or change him. Eventually, Harry began coaching David to get up on his own and walk to the bathroom beside his bedroom. It took a long time for David to make the connection, but we kept at it.

What a thrill it was the first night David got up and went to the bathroom on his own — with only the flush of the toilet and the slam of the lid to wake us and let us know what had happened! That became a welcome sound, nightly, for the rest of David's life; we were always grateful for this added level of independence.

David remained smaller than most premature children, so Dr. Thomas connected us with a pediatric endocrinologist to have his growth pattern assessed. The doctor recommended that we administer growth hormone injections, which we did for several months before discontinuing them. We all decided that the injections weren't necessary, since David did not realize that he was small. Would he have been small had my pregnancy gone to term? Some questions were unanswerable.

Sensory perception

Every few years we brought David to a local ophthalmologist to have his eyes assessed. The doctor believed David's blindness prevented him from perceiving any light. Jared, Rachel, and Harry would often test this theory, quietly approaching David with flashlights and watching his reaction. David would usually think it was a great game and would yell that he could see the light. Since he was unable to explain precisely what he noticed, we wondered whether he did see fragments of light or whether he was responding to the warmth of the flashlight.

A careful listener, David learned to recognize the differences in our footsteps as we walked about in the house. Using his keen sense of smell, he could recognize each family member by our scent if he happened upon one of us before we spoke. Grabbing an arm and lifting it to his nose was a common habit of David's.

As he got older, upon meeting someone new, David would often ask eagerly, "Who are you?" While extending an arm toward the person, he would add, "I want a hand-touch." This is when Harry, Rachel, Jared, or I had to be prepared to run interference, gauging the person's ability to manage David's need to identify others with his hands, ears, and nose. Watching him overwhelm people with his curiosity could be entertaining, but we needed to keep a handle on appropriate behavior.

Public realities

When Jared was in the sixth grade, his teacher assigned writings on various feelings. One evening Jared came to me saying, "Mom, I've started writing this essay, but I can't come up with an ending." He showed me what he had written so far on the topic *I'm Embarrassed When . . . :*

> I'm embarrassed when we're in a public place like a restaurant, store, etc., and my brother (who is blind and mentally impaired) starts saying weird things really loud. He is really small but can talk very well and is also very smart.

It was a revelation to me to read this. I thought about it and acknowledged to Jared the reality of what he had written. We'd all had to come to terms with the difficulties of taking David out in public. When he was younger, it was easier — as his disabilities were less notable. But as he grew older, the stares, pointing, and questions became more common.

Being a reserved, private person, I had learned to armor myself with plans and self-talk for being in public with our attention-drawing son. Having worked hard with David on appropriate behavior, we were also trying to teach Jared and Rachel how to respond when difficult situations arose. I reminded Jared of this and of our family plan for those times when David acted out. Jared returned to his room to finish the essay.

I'll admit that I searched for the essay in Jared's backpack after he went to bed and eagerly read its conclusion:

> My mom always tells me to act calm and proud, and my dad says not to be embarrassed because I probably won't ever see those people again.

Work schedules

Given my everyday care for David, people often assumed I was a nurse. Nudged along by their comments and encouraged by Harry, I returned to school once Rachel was in preschool and in 1994 became a registered nurse. Nursing school gave me a deeper understanding of David, his present health, and the seriousness of his birth traumas. And, in turn, I developed greater empathy for others who suffered losses. I couldn't always fix their problems, but I was passionate about making things as good as possible for them in their present condition.

For several years I worked nights, and Harry managed David's morning routine, getting him ready for the school bus early. Arriving home after the household was off to work and school, I then slept during the day, getting up to help David off the bus around 2:30 p.m. Eventually I took a daytime job, and Jared, Rachel, Harry, and I coordinated our schedules so that one of us could meet David's bus. Neighbors told us that the sound of David's bus coming and going over the years let them know what time it was without looking at a clock.

When we had scheduling conflicts and needed someone to meet the school bus, our neighbor Wilma would watch for it and take David to her house. David came to love this woman, and she became an important person in our lives. Wise, older, and no-nonsense, she also was a big emotional support to me.

One autumn afternoon, after loading David into the car to go somewhere, I started the car and then ran back to the house to shut the door. I returned to a locked vehicle—with David inside. No way could he understand my pleas to unlock the door, so I called both the fire department and Wilma. Thankfully, David eventually unlocked the door, and after Wilma and I helped him out, she held onto both of us while I sobbed with fear and relief. The weight of David's dependence on us was sometimes overwhelming.

After that, we kept a spare key handy.

Gross motor skills

David learned to make his way around our house on his own, though he'd occasionally bang into things. At times, he preferred scooting on his rear end. When we were out and about with him, we tried to get him to use his white and red cane. Although his teachers worked with him on cane technique, he never appreciated or mastered the freedom a cane could give. With Sue, the mobility specialist at school, he sometimes cooperated. With us, throwing it suited him better!

David developed the ability to feed himself (albeit with his fingers). While we continued to encourage him to use his spoon and fork, we often wound up giving him a lot of help. Utensil skill, Harry and I realized, we probably did not promote enough. It took too much time and we were impatient. Usually we scooped each bite onto a spoon and let him do the rest.

Never a long-distance walker, David rode in strollers for years. As he outgrew traditional strollers, we investigated other types of chairs that would be more dignified and comfortable for him yet would go wherever we needed. Working with a medical equipment company, we tested several until settling on one made in England called a "pushchair." It was perfect—comfortable, sturdy, and easy to maneuver both through museums and over dirt trails.

Family camp

One summer we began attending an annual weeklong camp at a nearby lakeside conference center for families with children who have special needs. Throughout the week volunteers provided one-on-one fun and care for the children with special needs. Speakers brought daily encouragement to the parents, and siblings like Jared and Rachel had plenty to keep them busy too.

David loved this week and talked about it all year, always wondering who his next special helper would be. He took great pleasure in participating in Special Olympics–style events, each year choosing to compete in the 100-yard walk, the 100-yard run, and the chair race. For David, camp meant being pushed on the swings, having books read to him on the beach, listening to the waves of Lake Michigan, and racing throughout the grounds in his pushchair, propelled by strong young volunteers. For the rest of us, this week became a time to meet other families with unique members and to gain new insights and perspectives.

David's memory

David's memory for people, events, and facts (including trivia) soared, amazing and baffling us. He loved keeping track of things like our daily schedules, upcoming events, past experiences, and people. He remembered almost everyone he ever met and seemed to categorize them into family groups — so that when he came across one family member, he would immediately ask where each other member was, even if it had been years since he had last met them.

David associated everyone he met with an object. It varied whether he would connect people with their dog, their lawn mower, or the brand of vacuum cleaner they used — but once he knew, he never forgot. He loved music and could name the artist or band for most popular songs, with his brother and sister keeping him well supplied with music. Favorites were Eric Clapton (#1), Creedance Clearwater Revival, Bob Seeger, Jimi Hendrix, Bruce Springsteen, Steely Dan, and The Beatles. David could adjust the dial on his bedroom CD player on his own once someone else inserted the requested CD. Then he would sit in his beanbag chair and listen, or return to his bed, bouncing on the mattress in time to the music.

Rachel and Jared became David's greatest friends and teachers. He kept close track of their schedules and friends, and loved being part of their lives. During high school, Jared and his friends often took David to the bowling alley, where he was in his element listening to the rolling balls and crashing pins.

An adept conversationalist

David enjoyed engaging in conversation and could extend almost endlessly a thought or question that interested him. We were fascinated with his ability to manipulate the direction of a conversation *and* with his persistence in sticking to the point he wanted to discuss.

Simple, silly things captivated him. Entire drives to get his hair cut twenty-five miles away could revolve around the question, "Dad, what kind of a man is Joel?" (Joel was David's barber, and when he moved his business out of town, we followed him because we didn't want to search for a replacement.) Harry, loving to play this game with David, would announce that Joel was the mayor, or Joel was a builder, or perhaps Joel was a fireman. With each answer, David would roar with laughter and ask again, waiting for Harry finally to give the answer he was waiting for. OK, Joel was a barber. This would please David immensely, causing him to bounce in his seat and rock the entire car. He was an exuberant bouncer. More than once this caused non-family members riding with us to ask whether everything was all right with the car. "Look in the back seat," we'd say with a smile.

Egg cartons

Egg cartons became one of David's favorite topics of conversation. But only Styrofoam, please! We never knew why — perhaps it was the squeak of the Styrofoam. Many innocent people would be drawn into David's net with questions such as, "Do you like eggs? Do you make omelets? What kind of egg carton do you have? Where do you get your egg cartons?" For fear someone might have, or bring, a cardboard carton.

Although many good people over the years saved their egg cartons and proudly delivered them to David, the acquisition of an egg carton held his attention only for a moment. For David, the joy was in the quest: Do you have one?

He maintained his interest in egg cartons all of his life. Whenever visiting at friends' homes, the inevitable questions would come: "What can you bake? Do you have eggs?" He would thrill to hear the creak of the carton, the crack of the eggs, and the whir of the mixer. At home all I would have to do is open the refrigerator and take out the eggs, and he would yell from wherever he was, "Mom, what are you making?"

One evening Jared was home with David while the rest of us were out. While teaching a guitar lesson in the living room, Jared heard an unusual sound coming from the kitchen, so he paused the lesson and went to investigate. There sat David on the kitchen floor, in front of the refrigerator, an open egg carton in his hands and a mischievous look on his face. Some eggs were intact; others lay cracked on the floor. This was the only time David ever pursued his egg-carton fascination on his own, and (despite the mess) we found joy and some pride in the fact that he'd taken matters into his own hands.

Woodchips and spatulas

Woodchips and shredded bark also fascinated him. He liked the texture, the smell, and the word itself: *woodchips*. Having a load of woodchips delivered to our driveway every May was one of the highlights of his year. In the spring of 2003 we decided to spread woodchips over a large area of our backyard where grass didn't thrive. This became a favorite place for David. He spent hours in the woodchips that summer — sitting, lying, and rolling in them as he listened to airplanes, birds, neighborhood lawn mowers, and children playing. All the while he would flick woodchips between his fingers.

One of us would keep an eye on him, often sitting in a nearby glider reading or doing homework. But we had to reassure neighbors that David was there by choice — he wasn't being ignored or neglected!

Woodchips weren't the only things David would flick between his fingers. David learned to do amazing rotations of objects in his hands. Spatulas, pencils, pens, and pastry brushes all worked well. We'd never dare be in the car or in a public place without an item for him to flick between his fingers. The action distracted and calmed him.

David loved motion — being pushed high on a swing, riding in a cart behind a bike, sliding down the driveway on a sled, speeding down the lake in a boat, or tubing behind a boat with Rachel or Harry. Yet he also loved a gentle breeze, loved running his fingers through the water as he sat quietly in a kayak with Jared, Harry, or Grandma Knol.

Pineapple

David developed a fascination with several words that began with the letter P: pudding, pretzels, popcorn, and pineapple. All became favorite foods to eat — except pineapple, which he really liked just for the sound of the word, and perhaps for the smell. Once he realized that pineapple can come in several forms, his obsession became so intense we had to declare Saturday (and only Saturday) "Pineapple Day" for many years. All week he would debate what type he would want that week — tidbits, slices, chunks, fresh, or juice. On Saturday, the day of decision, the entire week's anticipation would peak when a can would be opened and its contents emptied into a bowl placed before him. Carefully he would touch, smell, and sometimes lick it, but generally not eat it.

Pineapple! Nothing pleased David more than to receive pineapple — for his birthday, in his Christmas stocking, in his Easter basket, from a friend. Once he received a fresh pineapple from Hawaii, personally delivered by friends of ours. His fascination with the word *Hawaii* provided as much delight as the pineapple itself. He came to insist that we read each pineapple can label "to see where it came from." Hanging on our every word, he would wait for us to say "Hawaii," which we learned always to include.

Rachel wrote a book for David entitled *Pineapple*. Having done her research, she could now read to David about how and where pineapples grew. Of course she also included what forms pineapple came in; for David, this was always the most important information. Sometimes we would omit that part intentionally, just to enjoy his reaction. When we heard that pineapple was being introduced in the form of stars and other new shapes, I went out and bought some, but David was not impressed. He wanted nothing to do with them.

I rarely brought David to the grocery store, but one Saturday he came with me to select the pineapple of the week, which this time was juice. I searched the aisles but couldn't find any, so I asked an employee, who told me it was out of stock. Just as he was saying there might be some in the backroom, David grabbed and scratched the poor man, angry at the prospect of going without pineapple juice. Horrified and apologetic, I got David under control and worked on a quick exit. The employee soon caught up with us and handed me a large can of pineapple juice, warming my distraught heart and absolutely delighting David.

"Kaboom"

When David was very young, a visiting friend began playing a silly game that David enjoyed. The two of them would slap each other's hands and call out "Kaboom" every time their hands met. Years went by, and we lost touch with him. But one day David, with his fantastic memory, remembered this person and the game. He began playing a variation of it in which he clapped his hand anywhere on another person's body and yelled, "Kaboom!"

This became another obsession, which again sometimes led people unwittingly into an activity they didn't know how to handle or escape from. No matter how hard Harry and I tried to keep the game in check, David mischievously found ways around us.

David's delight with "Kaboom" reflected the joy he generally found in high-energy play. He would howl with laughter when others would goof around rambunctiously and get themselves into trouble, and his sense of humor was contagious.

Bath-time routines

David needed help with bathing, as with all of his personal care. Over time he came to love his baths. Soaking in a warm tub gave him comfort and pleasure. In his teens, he learned to undress himself and climb into the tub on his own, once we had his bathwater ready. After one of us washed him, he could get out of the tub by himself and do a semi-effective job of drying himself. With pull-on clothes laid out on the counter, he began to dress himself. The clothing may have been put on backwards or inside out, but we were thrilled with his independence, and David was happy to be in control. Adjustments were later made with his clothing if we happened to be going out.

Clothing with buttons didn't work for David — he would just get frustrated and yank the buttons off. We also found that any fabric he could pick at would be unraveled in no time, so we intentionally kept his clothes simple. On Sundays he would occasionally tolerate a button-down shirt and a sweater, but only if he were allowed to remove them right after church.

Jared and Rachel helped with David's bathing. When Rachel was in her early teens, Harry suggested that perhaps it was time for Rachel to stop bathing her adolescent brother. He talked to her about it one evening, thanking her for her willingness to help but explaining that since David's body was maturing she could stop helping at bath time.

What? Rachel let Harry know that this was a silly notion and that she would continue helping David right along with the rest of us. She marched David into the bathroom, started the water, and bathed him — and continued for the rest of David's life.

In his late teens, David found he liked taking showers. Then, in typical David fashion, he began obsessing about needing a shower, telling us how dirty he was. The problem was, once he was in the shower, it was hard to get him out. Harry and I realized that we certainly put out money for activities Jared and Rachel enjoyed, so why not allow David to stand (and sit) in the shower for as long as he wanted? But no more than once a day!

Clothing, style, and color

It was always important to us that David look good. We made sure his clothing was in fine shape and always checked before we left the house to make sure he was clean and well groomed. First impressions are largely visual, and with David's unique characteristics, we wanted him to look impeccable. We had his hair cut regularly and always had a routine of wetting and combing it before he left the house. David was used to this and even reminded us to do it if we forgot. Shaving David, once he hit his mid-teens, became a whole new multi-sensory experience for all of us.

Because he was small, others often misjudged his age. Rachel and Jared became David's advocates in making sure his clothes were age-appropriate. I would never remove price tags until the items had passed their inspection.

David loved talking about colors and asking what color things were. It became a bit of a problem when he began asking people, even strangers, what color *they* were. We remedied this by reminding David to ask what color eyes or shirt or hair they had. Since his favorite color was red, that was always the answer he hoped for.

Friends were intrigued by David's fascination with color and often asked what we thought he imagined color to be. We thought his joy came simply from hearing the variety of answers. Twister was one of his favorite games, and he would lie on the mat happily slapping a hand, foot, elbow, nose, ear, chin, or tongue in response to whatever color and body part we yelled out.

Imitations and impersonations

With his keen ear, David was great at doing imitations. Dogs were his specialty. It was hilarious to watch dogs respond by darting back and forth, looking for the source of the barking. One day David was imitating a random sound, and when we finally asked him what he was doing, he announced he was eating an apple — and the sound was exactly right. His trumpet imitations were amazing, as were his impersonations of various family friends.

David's Grandma Knol, an immigrant from The Netherlands, sang Dutch songs and recited a Dutch prayer to all of her grandchildren when they were young. But it was David who mastered them, learning to reproduce the words so perfectly that even native Dutch speakers couldn't detect an accent. Curiously, David didn't seem to notice his grandparents foreign accent, but he was always excited when they entertained Dutch friends and he could hear the language spoken.

While David eagerly anticipated doctor appointments, surviving the minutes in the waiting room with him was always interesting. During the drive to the appointment I would review appropriate waiting-room behavior and, always quick with an answer, he would announce that he knew he needed to whisper, not talk loud. Yet without fail, once we were seated in the waiting room, David would, after listening to the people sitting around him, begin to imitate one of them, child or parent. The more emotional a child or adult became, the happier David would be, as he either continued his impersonation or joined in their conversation. Meanwhile there I would sit, trying to look nonchalant and reminding David to whisper. It really was quite funny, but only rarely did someone smile at me, enjoying David's uniqueness.

In and around water

At our small getaway cottage on an inland lake in northern Michigan, David rode in kayaks, canoes, speedboats, and pontoon boats most summers. Since he wasn't confident alone in the lake, we usually had a head-supporting life jacket for him. When he outgrew the child-size versions, we worked for months with a sporting goods store to find a larger alternative.

He loved being on or near water and often asked to float on his back. One of us would position him in the water and assure him that his life jacket would support him. But David always insisted on still holding someone's hand and, while floating, would inevitably burst out singing Christmas songs.

He came to insist on having a towel over his head whenever he sat in a fast-moving boat. Why, we never knew, but he always asked if we had a towel for him, and we all got used to seeing him sitting in a boat with a towel over his head and a spatula in his hand. Newcomers to the lake would delicately ask what *that* was all about.

Milestones

We celebrated David's birthday every year but hosted large celebrations every five years, on David's fifth, tenth, and fifteenth birthdays. Lots of family and friends eagerly celebrated his life and their love for him. Even Linda, his delivery room nurse, attended his birthday open houses, marveling at the life he lived. Although his birth had set us on course for a different life than we had anticipated, his birthday became a joyful day of thanks for the individuality that defined David.

Despite all the progress David made, he never got out of a car without our help. He couldn't have left the house on his own in case of a fire. He never grasped the concept of answering a ringing telephone. And the idea of getting food when he was hungry never occurred to him.

He also never recognized the disabilities others saw in him.

Because David became so comfortable with himself, we were able to see him whole, just the way he was. He had come to a place in life that was secure and happy. He thrived on routine, consistency, and stability. And though he frustrated us all regularly, he loved us unconditionally, as we loved him.

ages sixteen through nineteen:
evidences of grace

"Friends of David"

Planning and scheduling care for David took a great deal of effort, even though it was something we were long accustomed to. Grandparents and friends helped out often. But in the fall of 1999, it became clear that we had outgrown many of the young people who had been comfortable caring for David, and we were increasingly having a hard time finding caregivers. It was requiring more phone calls to find someone able to watch him. At the same time, Jared left for college and Rachel entered high school, making them less available.

When our friend Diane became aware of this, she stepped in and formed a respite team called "Friends of David." From then on, the friends Diane recruited met at our home each January for a planning party. At the end of the evening we'd have a list of three families per month that we could call on to watch David for a few hours at a time when we needed to be somewhere without him.

Since he was ever curious, David preferred going to these families' homes over having someone stay with him at our house. All he really required was a sofa where he could hang out, flick a spatula and listen to music — or to a mixer, a vacuum, or even the washer, dryer, or refrigerator. It all sounded new and different to him, and the varying levels of activity in these houses fascinated him.

Each year, as word got around, new names were added to the Friends of David respite list. This became a wonderful source of enrichment in David's life, as well as a tremendous help and encouragement to the rest of us. At our yearly sign-up gatherings, friends eagerly shared experiences and insights David had given them.

Planning the future

Knowing we wanted to keep caring for David but realizing the uncertainty of the future, Harry and I began talking about group home possibilities for David. When Rachel goes to college, we thought — perhaps this could be a natural transition and a good time for David to move into another care setting. Our idea was to get David's care well established and to monitor it closely, with Jared and Rachel also aware of the long-term responsibility we all felt towards him.

We began exploring places, found a setting that closely fit our criteria, and put David's name on a waiting list. Rachel, who was in high school at the time, made it clear that she could not bear the idea of coming home from college without David present. "There will be enough change already," she said. "I'll need to find David at home. Can't we wait until I am adjusted to college, maybe until my sophomore year?"

A new church

In 2000 we started attending a different church. At first unsure of how people there would react to David, we were pleased to find that all five of us were warmly welcomed. The education director immediately asked us what the congregation could do for David. Since David sat well during worship services, we wanted to continue that routine in this new church, which was comfortable for him. And we figured that if we always sat in the same area to worship, anyone who might be distracted by David's flicking a pen or spinning his head could decide to sit elsewhere.

We did explore a mid-week spiritual class for developmentally disabled adults called Friendship Ministries. Upon investigation, we discovered that David could join a Friendship Class that met on Tuesday evenings at another local church. The program requested that our home church provide a one-on-one assistant for David. Dreading to ask for help in a new church, we eventually told our church's education director about the program and asked whether she knew of anyone who might be willing to attend with David. Jolynn stepped forward and began working with him each week. The class involved singing, prayer requests (a big deal), a Bible story, a craft, and a snack (another big deal). David loved attending, and Friendship became a highlight of his week. It was exciting for the rest of us to drop him off for an activity on his own, independent from us.

Alarm

Harry occasionally reminded me that David could develop health problems related to the liver, kidney, and intestinal trauma sustained during his neonatal experience. I chose not to think about these things, deciding I would deal with whatever came up when it did, and not before. A coping skill I'd developed, this protective measure kept me from being overwhelmed with David and his daily care.

One evening in early 2001, after a routine physical exam earlier in the day, Dr. Thomas telephoned us to explain that lab results indicated David's kidney function was deteriorating. Some slippage had been noted in 1999, but the decline was now severe. Dr. Thomas reminded me of the kidney damage David had sustained during his early days. He explained that we would have serious decisions to make in light of this decline and that he would remain an active participant in care and in decision-making about how aggressive the treatment should be.

We were shocked by the news. David did not appear ill — in fact, after his difficult first years, he had become the healthiest member of our family. But kidney disease, we discovered, is silent in its early stages.

Occasionally, throughout David's life, friends had asked us about his life expectancy. For years David had been very healthy, so we felt that his life expectancy was as good as any of ours. We lived well, had good routines with David and his care, had an adequate support system, and did not feel that our lives were stifled because of him.

Having dealt with kidney failure in patients I'd encountered in my work as a nurse, I knew this news was not good. Memories of David's traumatic birth and frustrating early years haunted me as I vividly recalled the pain and confusion he had endured. Could we once again require him to experience things he would not understand?

We met with a kidney specialist, a nephrologist. Ultrasound revealed that David only had one kidney. Maybe we should have already known this from his NICU days, but somehow that fact had bypassed Harry and me. After reviewing David's lab results, and hearing of our desire to maintain David's current quality of life, the doctor told us it was hard to tell what these labs meant for the future. He did not feel that monitoring David closely was necessary yet.

We shared this unsettling information with family and close friends, but life went on in normal fashion. It didn't seem necessary to share the news with others, since we were uncertain ourselves what the future held. Waiting to see what would develop, we wondered how we would respond if the disease progressed.

"My Jesus, I Love Thee"

The Friendship Class leader and our church's education director began prodding us to have David make a public statement of his faith. This is often done in our denomination when a person feels ready to make a faith commitment. Harry and I didn't know how this could work for David, who had a simple faith in God; we didn't want to expose him to a public situation that he could not handle. We were given a book on the importance of including those with cognitive impairments in the full life of the church, and we began discussing the idea with Jared and Rachel. Jared initially felt it was inappropriate to put David through this process. Yet, the more we learned about how the process could be tailored to David's situation, the more comfortable we all became. Yet Jared set one criterion: If David were to go through this process, it could not be a circus — or cute.

In October 2002, David went with Jolynn to talk with our pastor and the elders of our church about his faith. I brought him to the meeting but waited outside the room, having learned long before that people reacted more naturally to David if they didn't have to all the while worry about me. From my place in the hallway, I could hear everything clearly. David, recognizing our pastor's voice, quickly became comfortable and asked, "Jack, do you know that Halloween is coming up?" Jack enthusiastically assured David that he did know, and agreed with him about what a fun day that was. Then he asked David whether he loved God and liked coming to church. David readily said yes. When Jack asked David if he wanted to mention a favorite song, David instead burst out singing all the verses of the hymn "My Jesus, I Love Thee." The others in the room were spellbound, many brought to tears. Out in the hallway, I was amazed at this son of mine, with his pure, spontaneous responses.

I was then invited to enter the room, where we all held hands and sang the doxology, "Praise God, from Whom All Blessings Flow." David, now realizing there were several people in the room, wanted to know all of their names. He listened intently to each name and interacted briefly with each person. The education director then presented David with a tray of fresh pineapple chunks for him to enjoy with the group.

On November 17, 2002, David stood before the congregation with our pastor and publicly stated his belief in God. He recited John 3:16 from the Bible and after some hesitation decided to again sing "My Jesus, I Love Thee." As he stood there, embracing and hanging onto our pastor, he conducted himself with astonishing confidence.

This event took place a month before his twentieth birthday. In attendance were members of our church, our family, and several close friends, including Dr. Thomas, and Linda, the delivery room nurse who had been following his progress for twenty years. It was an evening of incredible beauty and love.

Dropping Braille

One of the things I fretted about early in David's life was whether Harry and I should learn Braille. When David's school began introducing pre-Braille concepts early on, I tried to determine when we should start enhancing that instruction at home — but, truthfully, I was too busy with the three kids and lacked the energy to pursue it. Instead, I decided to monitor how David was doing with Braille at school and planned to dive in and start learning it the minute I saw him making good strides. This seemed a sensible solution, though I did feel some guilt over it from time to time.

David loved the Braille machine at school, and we knew about the concepts the teachers were working on. At each parent-teacher conference, we would pay close attention to David's Braille progress, and year after year we were told that David had to master the concepts of right/left and upper/lower before he could get anywhere with Braille.

Those were concepts we could work on at home. David was a good sport and at times seemed quite sure of left/right. But just when we thought he was grasping the concept, we came to realize he was happily answering randomly.

Shortly before David turned twenty, his teachers asked, with some trepidation at a parent-teacher conference, whether Harry and I might agree to drop Braille from David's goals. Permission granted, I chuckled to myself as I realized that years earlier we had saved ourselves tremendous effort and frustration by allowing David to lead us.

David remained with the same teacher and students at school for many years. His backpack always contained a small notebook. Notes were written back and forth almost daily between staff reporting on David's day and we informing them of any pertinent information. Harry and I attended twice-a-year parent-teacher conferences, and not usually much in-between. Once in a while, we tried to enjoy some evening event the school hosted, but this only proved frustrating and confusing to David. Coming to school with us at night, completely out of what he considered normal routine for school, produced a lot of agitation and anxiety. No fun for any of us. So we found other ways to support the school.

After David had been with his teacher, Cheryl, for many years, she confessed to us how concerned she had been initially when David joined her class. By that time Harry was a Special Education Teacher Consultant,

travelling throughout the public school district. How
would she possibly keep this family satisfied? She
recalled that at our first parent-teacher conference with
her, she asked what our goals for David were. When
we, and especially Harry, responded that our goal was
for David to be happy and feel safe at school, Cheryl,
unbeknownst to us, breathed a huge sigh of relief. Her
creativity, joy, sensitivity, and insight made school
a second home for David, where he found friends,
developed new skills, and expanded his world.

"Green-chair talks"

Occasionally, David would have bursts of frustration
or anger over things he could not understand, and
we would physically have to control him. This was
especially true as he grew older. Once, he and I joined
some friends at a restaurant. Seeing it was crowded, I
realized that the situation was risky, but David wanted
to be there. As we were being led to a table, David was
startled by someone's loud laugh and responded by
grabbing and scratching the friend walking ahead of
us. Surprised, she screamed, and I brought an out-of-
control David right to the ground to try to calm him.
Not having the energy to deal with the friend too, I
asked her to go on, saying I would catch up.

I had learned in situations like these not to make
eye contact with anyone, but to try calmly to get David
back in control. This required a tremendous amount of

strength and emotional energy. It worked best when we asked David himself to tell us when he was ready to be in control again. And he would. Whatever had set him off, he just needed a bit of time to calm himself down again. On the other hand, our responsibility was to try to avoid over-stimulating, anxiety-producing situations.

Our emotions during such public encounters varied with how others responded. Some people were more helpful than others, and we did all we could to avoid scenes. Not everyone was flexible enough or emotionally equipped to know instantly how to react when unexpected situations occurred. We were always on guard in public, having long learned that with David, anything could happen. Those who could quietly stand by, support, and stay calm with us were the most helpful.

It was a good thing David didn't understand that by this time he was only a little smaller than I was. Occasionally, at a family meal, David wouldn't be able to stop a tantrum from erupting. We would give him several chances to improve his attitude, but if that did not happen, Harry or I would lead him away from the table to his bedroom, just off the eating area. Now, this was not what he wanted — being removed was his worst punishment — so it was never a pretty sight, me leading him and David fighting, feet dragging and arms flailing. Yet within minutes of his exile, he would timidly re-approach the family and genuinely ask one of us for forgiveness.

Rachel was often at the receiving end, and sometimes she would begrudge his apology. "He'll just do it again some other time — I know it!" Hitting, kicking, and pinching produced a stronger reaction from her than from Jared. We worked to help her understand that she had every right to be angry with David when his behavior was inappropriate, and that, yes, he would do it again and she should be prepared. But his apologies were also so real — *at that moment* he felt truly remorseful for what he had done. At times, if he brought Rachel or someone else to tears, David too would start crying, even sobbing, which would remind us of his inability at times to control his behavior. These occasions made for many heart-breaking moments for each of us.

David and I both needed time-outs once in a while, so I developed what I called "Green-Chair Talks." If he had been frustrated for longer than usual, I would declare that it was time for a Green-Chair Talk and lead him by the arm to a quiet room, where he would sit on my lap as I quietly, calmly held him close. Just as often I was the one in need. Feelings of sadness or of being overwhelmed with David's dependence and care would lead me to require this – a quiet time of regrouping, of talking softly with him or just holding him. These times did not last more than ten or fifteen minutes, but the break helped each of us refocus and renewed our strength.

Learning what's important

We were always aware of how others interacted with David, and usually it was obvious from the start whether a person would be comfortable with David or not. Those who were comfortable became hands-on immediately, eagerly interacting with him, much to David's delight. Others, we came to recognize, enjoyed getting to know him from a distance. However, the love that friends and relatives had for David could be felt regardless of their comfort level in interacting with him. Sometimes with David it was *come closer at your own risk!* But it was always worth the risk.

Rachel began bringing home a new boyfriend whom David immediately latched onto. John, trying to be polite and figure David out, wasn't sure how to react to how physical David wanted to be. That didn't matter to David — or stop him from teaching John how things worked in our household. David adored him. When John asked if he could help feed David, I knew my daughter had found a good person.

Late one afternoon in the spring of 2003 I received a call from John. Rachel, he said, couldn't make it to a concert they were planning to attend that evening. Would I like to come along instead? It was already 5:00 p.m., and Harry wasn't due home until late that evening.

Thanking him for his kind invitation, I said I wouldn't be able to find someone to take care of David on such short notice.

Minutes later the phone rang again. It was John. His college roommate, he announced, was willing to come over and watch David. Joe had heard about David but had never interacted with him. David, always eager to meet someone new, was thrilled with the idea, so I agreed and called Harry to tell him about the plan.

When Harry returned later that evening, he found the house empty. Looking outside, he found David sitting in the dark in a patch of woodchips, happily discussing them with his new friend. David had been asking for woodchips, so Joe figured they might as well go outside and find some. Then David had insisted on sitting in them, so there they were, talking together about woodchips and about the sounds they were hearing. Joe's kindness and perceptiveness amazed us.

When Jared and Rachel were away at college, finding David was their first priority whenever they came home to visit. Pouncing on him, wrestling, hugging, or reading to him delighted David as much as it did them.

Reflecting on the prayers Harry had initiated years before, our hearts were full of thanks for the happiness we saw shining through David. To him life was great — and so it was. He became a confident, cheerful, curious — and opinionated — young man who loved God's creation and shared his faith and life simply with others.

The light of God's love and grace shone through David as we cared for him. We learned from him what was truly important in life and were allowed to explore and understand more fully what life should be. He showed us how to live.

protecting david

Becoming very serious

In the fall of 2003, when David was twenty, things
suddenly became very serious. Not that we had
been ignoring the kidney disease, but to this point
the changes had not been significant. Now David
was exhibiting several symptoms indicating further
progression of the disease. Recognizing our desire to
consult a more specialized nephrologist, Dr. Thomas
told us about a pediatric nephrologist who had recently
begun practicing nearby. Even though David's age was
beyond the usual range of a pediatric specialist, this
nephrologist, Dr. Smith, agreed to monitor David,
since his kidney disease was related to damage as a
neonate.

Throughout that fall, we noticed that David was
sleeping more than normal. Jared and Rachel grasped
the seriousness of David's condition and began coming
home often, very concerned. Jared had graduated from
college in the spring and was living nearby, working in
medical research and planning to begin medical school
the following June. Rachel was a freshman in a nearby
college, living on campus.

Each of us wondered where this path would
lead. I felt that David could not tolerate dialysis or a
transplant but realized I needed to allow Harry, Jared,
and Rachel to reach their own conclusions.

Harry, David, and I met with Dr. Smith in October,
greatly pleasing David, who was always ready to meet

a new doctor. After reviewing David's history and labs, Dr. Smith told us that the situation was grave. David had perhaps one year to live. We could hardly grasp this news.

Fatigue, the doctor reminded us, is a silent symptom of kidney disease and it would increase over time. Frightened, we were also relieved to have a specialist monitoring David closely — and were pleased that it was someone who communicated with us freely and honestly.

David himself actually loved the new routine of going to the doctor every few weeks and enjoyed having blood work done. He listened closely, taking in facts and bits of information, all without seeming to comprehend that something serious was going on. For David no heavy emotional weight seemed to be attached to any of this; he eagerly added these doctor visits to his social calendar. Dr. Smith suggested that lab work be done in the same building where his office was. Maybe he thought this would be convenient. Well, after two times of that routine David made it very clear that he wanted to return to the long-familiar lab near our home. So we did. The name of the lab, Quest Diagnostics, fell into his category of fun-sounding words and he always anticipated greeting their familiar staff.

Lab results did not improve. Dr. Smith presented the three options we faced: dialysis, kidney transplant, or palliative care — focusing on comfort and the treatment of symptoms. David was in end-stage kidney failure — heartbreaking words.

We monitored David's eating carefully, avoiding foods harmful to the kidney. Kidney failure also brought bone loss, and medication was prescribed to strengthen David's bones and prevent fractures. Our job was to help keep him from falling. In consultation with the medical team, we agreed that David would have great difficulty with hospitalizations, and we decided together to work diligently to keep him monitored at home.

The options

One afternoon in early November, after David had come home from school, he announced that he wanted to listen to water. I suggested a drive to a nearby lake and he agreed. A few minutes later, as I was gathering my things in another room, I heard David tumbling down the basement stairs. Terrified, I ran toward the stairway and caught up with him just as he landed at the bottom. Startled but talking, he said, "Wow . . . I fell."

I began checking him over and, cell phone in hand, called Harry, who listened as I checked his whole body for pain or broken bones. Amazingly, David felt no pain and had no injuries other than a small scrape on his forehead.

Once he and I had settled down, David insisted that we carry out our plan to hear the wind and water — so off we went, my head still whirling. David did not usually walk in that part of the house by himself, and the door to the basement was always closed. I surmised that in his eagerness to get ready he may have mistaken that door for the bathroom door.

Since learning of the kidney failure, we had become extra protective of David, working hard to avoid falls. Now, in an instant, it had happened. As I sat by the lake with David that afternoon, I realized I needed to relinquish control and allow God's timing and plan to evolve.

I told Dr. Thomas about the fall and asked whether any tests should be done. If David was getting around, he said, and wasn't complaining of pain, there was no need. We watched David closely that night and for the next few days. No injury emerged.

Jared, Rachel, Harry, and I had ongoing discussions about the medical options we faced and what each scenario would mean for David. A decision had to be made very soon, we were told. Because Jared and Rachel had always been a vital part of David's life, they insisted, and Harry and I agreed, that the four of us should make all of David's medical decisions together. Their insight and opinions were valuable to everyone involved. An attempt would be made for each of us to accompany David to all doctor appointments. We all concluded that David's quality of life had to be maintained at the level he was accustomed to.

When David had turned eighteen two years earlier, Harry and I had gone to probate court to retain legal guardianship. Now the weight of being responsible for one who couldn't make important decisions for himself fell heavily on us.

I called and met with every medical professional I knew, talking with them about David's condition and the decisions we had to make. Everyone firmly indicated that with David's limited understanding and capabilities, it would not be right to put him through dialysis or a transplant.

A decision

A decision had to be made. Employed as a visiting nurse, I often had to pull over while driving around town, overwhelmed with sadness and fear as I constantly debated the options. With either dialysis or a transplant, I knew David would have to be restrained and sedated constantly — not only during the procedures, but all of the time, as he would not keep graft sites or IVs intact. With David, sores always took a long time to heal because he couldn't resist picking at them. We were never able to keep Band-Aids on him much longer than five minutes because he would pull them off, just as he would pull apart seams with loose threads or buttons on shirts.

Though Harry, Jared, Rachel, and I all agreed on a decision, we struggled nonetheless to put it into words. At our visit to Dr. Smith in December, he gently said, "As we've gotten to know David, we as a medical team feel it would be a disaster for this young man to go through dialysis or transplant. It could be done, but in our view it would be done for the benefit of the family and not for David."

We tearfully thanked him for his willingness to offer his candid judgment. It helped to know what these experts were thinking. By being willing to share the weight of a tremendously burdensome decision, they gave our family comfort, strength, and direction to proceed with the best decision we could make for our son and brother.

The doctor then explained what *could* be done to keep David comfortable and free of pain, and asked us to schedule a family meeting with him soon to discuss the decision. In addition, he said, we should bring to that meeting anyone in our family "who could be a problem" in the face of such a decision. The implications needed to be discussed fully so that everyone in the family would be on the same page. We were given information on hospice, and though I firmly believed in the concept, I found myself having trouble thinking of my own son in those terms.

We updated grandparents, uncles, aunts, cousins, and close friends. All voiced resolute support for maintaining David's high quality of life and sparing him anything he would not understand.

Dr. Smith explained that a letter would be sent to our home. It would state that David was in "the terminal phase of end-stage renal failure." We realized then that this letter — spelling out David's condition, the decisions made, and who had made them — was for the protection of both the doctors and ourselves. Another agonizing element had been added to the process.

It was necessary, we were advised, to keep the gravity of David's condition confidential within the circle of our family and close friends who knew and loved us, and who understood the agony of our decision. They would need to protect us from those unable to understand. At a time when we desperately needed support, we would also, ironically, need to build some fences.

Dr. Smith and Dr. Thomas each described cases in which a child under their care had unexpectedly died at home. Adding to the families' trauma were the police and coroner investigations that were required because of the place of death. Beginning hospice care earlier than we might feel necessary would provide an umbrella of safety, indicating that death was not unexpected and that appropriate care had been provided. No investigation would be necessary.

I couldn't sleep that night and finally went to David's room and rested beside him. He woke up, puzzled. "Why are you by my bed, Mom?" I let him know I just wanted to be close to him, and he tried to settle back down. Every few minutes he would say, "Leave!" Between tears and laughter, I tried to convince him I wouldn't stay long. He tossed and turned some more and finally commanded, "Mom, go back to your own bed!" I did, and actually slept.

When I got up the next morning, I walked first to his room and glanced at him, as I had done every morning since he was a baby. David always heard me, and that day he said, sleepily, "Turn on Sonshine Network" — a children's radio station that played religious songs and stories twenty-four hours a day. I turned it on softly and heard the words, "In his time, in his time, he makes all things beautiful in his time." I paused and listened. David, uncharacteristically, got up and stood beside me, also listening. He tipped his head to hear better, then softly sang along and whispered, "I like that song."

Acceptance

For the family meeting, held in February 2004, Harry, Rachel, Jared, and I met with Dr. Smith, his nurse, the pediatric social worker, and a social worker from a hospice agency. Talking with us for almost two hours, Dr. Smith thoroughly answered our questions and then offered his e-mail address for follow-up questions. He spoke to Jared and Rachel about how this experience would affect them for the rest of their lives.

Aware that Jared was heading to medical school in the summer, Dr. Smith told him, "In one year or in ten years or *any time* you have questions about decisions we made for your brother and you want to discuss them with me, I will be available for you." He then looked at Rachel and asked. "Rachel, how is it to be living in a college dorm with this going on in your life?"

The hospice social worker explained the kind of support hospice care could provide.

After reviewing again the details of dialysis and transplant, the four of us, together with the medical team, reaffirmed our decision that David would not be able to tolerate either.

At the end of the meeting, we asked when to schedule the next appointment. Dr. Smith responded that it wasn't necessary to return and that all lab blood draws could be stopped.

"No," Jared and I replied in unison.

With David's not looking ill, we needed to keep coming and we needed to keep seeing lab results — they brought reality to the situation, plus David enjoyed doctor visits and blood draws, I explained. Would he be willing to do that? Dr. Smith agreed to continue to work with us but cautioned that he would need our permission to provide the lab results as information only and to limit new medications to those that would enhance David's comfort. Thanking him for his willingness to continue monitoring David, we gave him the permission he requested.

Hospice care for David, we decided, would not be passive. On the contrary, we would actively do all we could to ensure that his every need was met.

We asked our pastor, Jack, to come to our home so we could discuss with him the gravity of David's condition. He had the right words and understanding. David was delighted to have this man in our home, one to whom he felt very connected, whose voice was the voice of church to him. Jack gave us a copy of a prayer by the Quaker leader William Penn:

> We give back to you, O God, those whom you gave to us. You did not lose them when you gave them to us, and we do not lose them by their return to you. Your dear Son has taught us that life is eternal and love cannot die. So death is only an horizon and an horizon is only the limit of our sight. Open our eyes to see more clearly, and draw us closer to you that we may know that we are nearer to our loved ones who are with you. You have told us that you are preparing a place for us, prepare us also for that happy place, that where you are we may also be always, O dear Lord of life and death.

Reassurance

Rachel, Jared, Harry, and I met with Dr. Thomas at his office early one evening. Having earned our trust over the years, he had insights and opinions about David's condition that were important to us; we each needed to hear from him. Dr. Thomas reflected on all that David had been through; on what David meant to him and to all of us; on what a remarkable young man he had become, far exceeding anyone's expectations; and on how remarkable he also would have been had my pregnancy gone to term. He said that being present at David's public profession of faith the previous year had been a highlight of his career.

Reassuring us, he affirmed that keeping David happy and feeling safe in the routines he knew was the best possible thing we could do for him.

Dr. Thomas spoke to Jared and Rachel about the love and care they gave their brother, emphasizing that David would continue to affect them in all they would do for the rest of their lives. We wept together as Dr. Thomas pondered with us, "What in the world are you people going to do without David?" Thankful for a compassionate doctor who had walked with us for twenty years, we were given strength and comfort to proceed.

David remained his happy, curious self. It was amazing to us that he seemed so normal while being so ill. He did lose some weight, and his color seemed to be off. Some days he slept a bit more than usual.

Friends and family began to protect us from people who would find it difficult to comprehend the extensive deliberations and agony involved in our decision. While thankful for the reassurance we received from family and friends who understood, we could not be reassured enough.

The hospice nurse and social worker assigned to David began visiting every couple of weeks, eagerly greeted by David, who enjoyed the routine of their visits.

Making the most

I met with our pastor in early spring 2004. I asked for his thoughts on the dying process, open versus closed caskets, memorial services, funerals, loss, and any other advice he could give me. He offered his thoughts on the questions I raised, and then said, "Faye, how you will grieve and miss David. But the people I have seen who grieve with hopelessness and despair are the ones who had unfinished business with their loved one."

These words set us on a course to live each day we still had with David in a way that would give us comfort for the rest of our lives. We tried hard to make the most of each day.

Jared moved home in March. He helped with David's care and took over most of David's bathing. They had great fun with the handheld showerhead, with David calling out what type of "shower bath" he wanted and Jared adjusting the nozzle to his requests and demands.

Jeff, a professional photographer who donates his services to pediatric hospice families, photographed our family. David was in fine form, enjoying every minute of the session and cooperating fully. In fewer than twenty minutes, some wonderful shots were taken — a triumph, since David was not easy to photograph. Jeff put him at ease.

David insisted on a certain routine at doctor visits. If he thought a step had been skipped, he would call out to remind us. Usually it was an insistence on having his temperature taken or on providing a urine sample: "Oh, we forgot — I need to pee in a cup!" At our March appointment as a nurse was taking his blood pressure, David insisted that he was doing great — "I don't have any kidney problems, I'm fine!"

What a roller coaster ride this was.

Harry, David, and I spent spring break at our cottage. David liked listening to Harry working on projects with power tools. Being near the Grand Traverse Bay, we often bundled up to go sit on the beach, feel the sand, and listen to the waves and seagulls.

It became clear to me during that week that I needed to take a family medical leave from work. As David's care and needs were changing by the day, I was becoming an unpredictable employee and was feeling torn. When I returned, my supervisor strongly encouraged me to spend time with David. "I'm not sure how long I will be off work," I admitted. She reminded me that even if I needed a year off, it would be time never regretted.

Wanting to take care of burdensome details, Harry and I made an appointment to select cemetery plots. We decided to purchase three as near to the grave of Harry's younger brother Jack as we could. Jack had died at age nineteen from a brain tumor, shortly after Harry and I had met. Through that experience my mother-in-law had gained tremendous insight, strength, and compassion, which she shared with me when David was born and throughout his life.

We also visited a funeral home and made prearrangements. It was emotionally draining, but we were relieved to know we had gotten through this painful process while we could think somewhat clearly. These decisions behind us, we quickly put them out of our minds.

One morning as David was trying to wake up and eat breakfast, he began singing, "He who began a good work in you, he who began a good work in you, will be faithful to complete it, will be faithful to complete it in you." I listened and wondered.

Certain friends began to check on us more frequently. Randy and Sheri, longtime friends, began providing many opportunities for us to share our feelings; often sensing our needs, they found ways to help before we ever had to ask.

David called out one night after midnight, "Can you lay by me?" I did, and noticed his body shaking slightly from time to time. A few minutes later, he said, "Leave now; go to your own bed." I did, returning about ten minutes later to check on him. I found him lying wide awake, quietly flicking his spatula. "Can you read *The Magic Blanket*?" he asked. It was a longtime favorite book.

Throughout the spring, David often asked to feel the sand. So we would head to Lake Michigan to sit, feel, and listen. He began asking me to sing lullabies before bed, something I had not done in years. He also started saying "I love you" more often to the four of us. Jared and Rachel thought it might be a ploy to get things he wanted — certainly possible with David, and often true — but he also said it more randomly and genuinely than ever.

I started driving David to and from school, avoiding the bus because, now that he was a hospice client, extra paperwork would have to be in place for him to continue riding. After so many years of loving the bus rides and his drivers, he surprisingly adapted quickly to the new arrangement.

People from my work asked what kinds of things David enjoyed and sent over a gift basket for him: books about trucks, pineapple in every form, popcorn, and gift certificates to McDonald's and other favorite restaurants. The presents were packed in woodchips.

"I need a little help"

David began asking for help in getting to places in the house he knew very well. "I need a little help. I'm kind of stuck," he would say, and we would find him sitting on the floor looking bewildered and disoriented. *Was this due to low hemoglobin, anemia?*

Our pastor called one day to see whether he could visit and asked what David liked to do. I told him our annual May woodchip delivery had arrived and that David had been spending a lot of time sitting outside. "Well," Jack asked, "could I come over and sit in the woodchips with David?" So there the two of them sat — listening to birds, lawnmowers, and airplanes while smelling, feeling, and talking about the woodchips.

A few people carefully asked whether we were preparing David by talking to him about dying. David did not need any more information that he could not understand; it would have just been something to obsess about. He loved the attention and care we gave him, that was enough.

School for David went year round, so I kept bringing him for a few hours a day. While he was there,

I ran errands, met with friends, or went walking at a botanical garden, a beautiful place near the school. This free time helped me keep my balance as David's care became more intense. After school David and I would often go to the new children's garden there. Using a wheelchair to cruise around, David and I could enjoy the outdoor water displays, chimes, and other sounds and smells.

At school the staff let him set the pace he could handle, as he continued to love the long-familiar school routine. His teacher, Cheryl, and the principal decided not to tell most of the other staff about David's illness, because they wanted life at school to be normal for him. Feeling he didn't need the extra attention his status could bring, we appreciated the privacy and their looking out for him. The hospice social worker came to talk to David's classroom staff and suggested books that could be helpful; she also helped them develop a plan of action in the event that David should have a crisis at school.

I felt the need to justify the fact that my son, who was dying, was still going to school. I mentioned this to Dr. Smith, who urged us to continue whatever routines were working and keeping David happy.

Rachel was living at home for the summer. Though working many hours, she also was very involved with David's care. Her presence and activity level kept David entertained, with her friends coming over often.

Jared was scheduled to start medical school in Nashville, Tennessee, that summer. This created mixed emotions for all of us — we were so unsure of how everything would play out. Jared spoke with Harry and me one evening, questioning whether he should be leaving. "Am I being selfish to leave now, with David so ill? Should I wait a year?" Having been such a vital part of David's life, he couldn't imagine being gone as this process unfolded. None of us could imagine it either. But Jared's life needed to continue. Dr. Thomas spoke with Jared and encouraged him to continue with medical school as planned.

In late June Jared left for Nashville and medical school. Harry, Rachel, and Rachel's boyfriend, John, went along to help him settle into his apartment while I stayed home caring for David, my emotions in turmoil. I hadn't the energy to spare to delve into what my oldest son's absence would mean for me.

Around this time Harry accepted a new position as head of special education and student services for a local school district. Hardly a time to take on a new job — but the opportunity came, and after eleven years as an elementary school principal, he was open to a change.

Relieved not to be employed at this time, I still felt the need to ease the coming crisis. I visited hotels and learned that many had bereavement rates, passing the information on to out-of-town family and friends so they could handle those details themselves when the time came.

Our cottage up north felt especially safe and comforting. We headed there as often as possible. As always, David loved the boat rides, woodchips, chirping birds, and all the activity on the lake. His fatigue was increasing, and he fell asleep often during the day. He found lying in the hammock and listening to the world around him relaxing and comforting. And as he relaxed, so could Harry and I.

The hospice nurse and social worker told us the cottage was beyond their territory, so we should have a plan for handling a crisis there should it arise. We figured that being there was worth the added risk; we would deal with whatever came up if necessary.

David constantly asked us to read to him, seeming to crave the chance to sit close together. We too found this comforting. One evening at the cottage, he called out from his bed, "Mom, how about you hold onto me and I'll hold onto you?" I rested by him and held him in my arms.

Late summer, 2004

David loved the cottage, but since we couldn't always be there and since he was always on a search for moving water, we also began driving to hear the waterfalls near the dam of the Rogue River several miles north of our home. By now we had a wheelchair of our own for David, and right by the falls was a park bench we would aim for. There we would sit for hours listening to the falls and reading his favorite books, soothed by the sound of the water.

Jared had a brief break from school in early August and came home for a visit. We were committed to getting him home at any opportunity.

The hospice nurse and social worker continued to come to our house every few weeks, offering a listening ear and support. Since I was not about to give up much of David's management and care, we talked and learned from each other.

One afternoon David called out, "My muscle mass hurts; my kidney hurts," pointing to his abdomen. "Do I have a kidney stone? It must be." His medical knowledge could be striking, and since someone he knew had had several bouts of kidney stones, he was familiar with the diagnosis. Self-diagnosing was something he had always attempted, fascinated as he was with doctors and illnesses. For example, when his eyes began watering and irritating him around this time, David said, "There's something the matter with the sparkle in my eye. I know what I need — new glasses." Oh, how he made us laugh — and made us realize again how closely he listened to the conversations around him.

After much discussion, Dr. Thomas and Dr. Smith — together with the four of us — decided to have

David begin taking iron in an attempt to alleviate his severe anemia, caused by the kidney failure. Fully aware that iron could cause further kidney damage, we all concluded that if iron would perhaps give David more energy, the risks would be offset by his enhanced quality of life.

I told Dr. Smith that the care we were giving David these days was not much different from what we were used to, so it was sometimes hard to realize how very ill he was. Dr. Smith reassured me that managing David was a full-time job and that by providing consistency in his routine and environment, we were helping him continue to thrive. When asked what he now thought David's time frame was, Dr. Smith softly said David would not be able to survive past midwinter.

Time was going by too quickly. We decided not to ask that question again.

September

By fall David's response to the iron was obvious — his energy level returned to near normal. It was amazing to see him once again wander about in the house on his own, to watch him walking back and forth to his CD player/radio, making adjustments by himself. David, too, seemed to notice that he was stronger; when asked how he felt, he repeatedly answered, "Better."

One afternoon he called out, "Mom, can we listen to 'The First Noel'?" I put in a Christmas CD, and David quickly skipped to the song he wanted. Then he yelled, "Mom, come hear 'The First Noel.' Want to hear the noel concert? Come! Have a seat. I love that 'First Noel'!"

Even though Rachel, now a college sophomore, had moved back to the dorm, she came often and was very concerned about all of us. She told us she was glad *not* to be living at home, though she felt some guilt over that. Yet she knew if she were living at home, she would be consumed with worry and care for David and wouldn't be able to keep up with her studies. Harry and I agreed that being able to come and go reduced the intensity of the situation for her. She was thankful to be at a local school so she could come home often.

October

In October my mom came from California for several days to help with David's care. Jared came home from Nashville for a short visit and did lots of wrestling with David. When I cautioned him against hurting David, he replied, "*I'm* the one you should be worried about," since David remained very strong. "But don't worry, Mom," he said, laughing, while he and David kept at it, "I know every one of his moves."

We reviewed all of David's medications with Dr. Smith mid-October. He made some adjustments and additions in response to David's occasional foot cramping and persistent eye discomfort.

It had been a year now since we realized that David's kidney condition was becoming serious and had begun seeing Dr. Smith. We reflected with Dr. Smith on what a good year David had had, how happy he remained, and how convinced we were that we were doing the best thing for him. Dr. Smith again reassured us, saying, "Dialysis or transplant would have been absolute cruelty for this young man." Then he said, "You people need to have a wonderful Thanksgiving this year."

David, however, had jumped ahead — he had already been talking about Christmas for a couple of weeks. Almost daily he insisted on being read a book about Jesus' being born in a manger, and he requested Christmas music during our car rides to school. When Dr. Smith spoke about Thanksgiving, David started singing, "Christmas is the time, Christmas is the time, Christmas is the time to love."

At a visit to the ophthalmologist later that day David received eye drops. As we were about to leave the exam room, the doctor paused, saw David flicking a pen, and asked, "*What* is that doing in his hand?" Quickly realizing the danger he perceived, I explained David's longtime need to "flick" something to keep himself calm and occupied, saying, "He never pokes himself in the eye with an object. And out in public a pen seems more appropriate than pastry brushes and rubber spatulas."

"Come now, certainly you are long past being concerned about what other people think! Go back to the pastry brush," the doctor pleaded. "That would be safer." By now we were both laughing. I would think about it, I told him.

November

My brother Charlie flew in from California to spend time helping us with David. During the visit David asked Charlie what kind of a man he was: "Are you a refrigerator man, Uncle Charlie?" This was one of David's word games, but people didn't always know what to do with it. Charlie knew. "No," he bellowed, "I am a FREEZER man, David!" David was thrilled that Charlie could think like he did. Lots of wrestling took place between the two of them.

David's hospice nurse took a new job, and we learned we were to receive interim help until a replacement nurse could be found. We would miss this nurse, as she had come to know and understand David well.

Occasionally David complained that his hands and feet felt "like ice cream" or were burning. Further, we began to notice again more fatigue and weakness. He would complain of being tired and would simply lie down wherever he was. We'd sometimes find him sitting on a kitchen stool with his head on the counter, sound asleep.

David's teachers noticed his increased fatigue too, and when they asked him whether he was all right, he would quickly sit up and say, "I'm okay." We began to decrease his time at school but still got him there for a few hours most days. The school nurses, whom we kept updated on David's condition, checked on him frequently.

Thanksgiving

David was thrilled to have Jared and Rachel home for Thanksgiving break. He produced lots of energy and showed almost no fatigue during their stay. After an early snowfall he even enjoyed wild sled rides in the yard with Jared.

On Friday the five of us went to select a Christmas tree. As always, David's goal was to hear the tree-shaking machine and smell the pine needles. Back at home, Jared and Rachel spent hours with David, wrestling, playing with his noisy toy animals, and reading books. Having heard that David enjoyed listening to the African drums at church, one of the church musicians brought them to the house for us to borrow. Jared and David had great fun playing the drums together.

Beginning when she was very young, Rachel often wanted to sleep by the Christmas tree and usually convinced David to sleep there with her. David came to think of this event as "sleeping in the manger" and brought it up each year once the tree was decorated. "Let's sleep in the manger!" he would say. Determined to sleep there the night of this year's tree arrival, he designated Jared as the one to join him. The rest of us went to bed with David in a sleeping bag by the Christmas tree, but we left a note for Jared, who was out with friends, explaining David's plan.

Sure enough, I awoke the next morning to find both of my sons asleep beside the tree.

Early December

I had mixed emotions about the approaching Christmas holidays. Our world had stopped, so it was surreal to watch normal life going on all around us.

A cousin of mine called one morning from her home in Arizona. We had grown up together and had always stayed close. Ready to hear anything I wanted to say, she was checking in weekly now to see how David and the rest of us were doing. Today I spoke with her about what December had become for me — a month full of memories of David and things he loved. To tread through this month with such pain in our hearts would be a delicate balancing act — remembering David's birth, hoping to celebrate his twenty-second birthday, recalling David's love of the Christmas season. Her empathy and compassion renewed my spirit.

The school staff reported that David continued to eat well for them. Since he was eating less for us, it was good to know he ate well there. His new eccentric food cravings at home became interesting. Often he would ask for pudding and then eat the whole batch. We gave him whatever he wanted. Popcorn, ice cream, and Reese's peanut butter cups were some of his favorites. Many evenings he decided that a McDonald's hamburger and french fries would help him feel better, so out Harry would go to get some. He would eat every bite and then relax in our recliner late into the evening, wrapped in Harry's arms.

Our pastor came to visit one afternoon in early December, thrilling David. As Jack sat by David's bed, talking with him, he held David's hand and then asked God to allow David to celebrate another birthday and one more Christmas with his family. After the prayer, David, ever the host, and luring Jack into staying awhile, asked, "Jack, do you want a cup of tea? My mom has tea!"

"I love tea — that would be great," Jack answered. At first David chose to stay in bed but then announced that he did want to join us at the table, so Jack led him. David was quite lively, talkative, and happy. He sat right beside Jack, grabbed his hand, sniffed it, and kissed it. He told Jack that he and I were off to the car wash and the pharmacy next.

Having always functioned better with plans, David stayed true to himself.

That evening David talked to Jared on the phone. "David, do you need a blood draw at Quest Diagnostics?" Jared knew how much David loved to hear the name of the lab. "Yes!" David said.

"Okay, let's do it," Jared said. "Roll up your sleeve. Get ready for the little poke. Okay, here comes a little poke!" David, listening intently on the phone, rolled up his sleeve and then, laughing, said, "Poke!"

Jared asked, "Now, David, what kind of Band-Aid do you want?" David said, "Garfield." "No, David, not always Garfield, think of another," Jared said. So David announced, "Scooby-Doo." Jared, as each of us, tried to get David to stretch beyond the rote answers he tended to give.

Two friends came over one morning to join me for our annual Christmas lunch while David lay quietly in bed. I had considered canceling this luncheon, but since it was my turn to host, I figured it would be a good diversion. Keeping up a somewhat normal routine was helpful, even though it brought on mixed emotions and inner turmoil.

My longtime friend Sharon came later that day. Sharon and I grew up together in California and had both settled in Michigan as adults. Together we found strength as we bolstered each other through whatever life brought. Sharon knew all of my hopes and fears for David. She knew now, without our having to speak, how grave the situation was.

Harry came home after work with David's order of a hamburger and french fries. In the evening Dan and Sandy came over. We had met Dan and Sandy in the NICU when both of our fragile babies lived there. Our friendship had grown over the years as we encouraged each other through life's joys and challenges. These good friends were invested in us and in David. David adored them.

As we spent the evening together, each of us took turns checking on David, who wanted to stay in bed. Although he was calm and loved the attention, we all felt uneasy about his cough and irregular breathing. David asked Sandy, "What kind of a man is Dan?" Sandy responded, "David, aren't you going to ask me what kind of a lady I am?" So David asked, "Sandy, what kind of a lady are you?" Sandy said, "I'm a nurse lady!" Sandy told him it was her job to take people's blood pressure and pulse, so of course David wanted her to take his blood pressure. Having someone else verify the high readings I had been getting was helpful.

That night Harry and David slept by the Christmas tree.

Our friends Dave and Karen asked if we could meet them for an early breakfast one Saturday morning. We explained we couldn't get David out and moving that early, and instead invited them to our house for breakfast. Knowing they were coming, David popped out of bed early, talkative and eager for their arrival.

Dave, Harry's fly-fishing partner, and his wife Karen had become good friends to us shortly after David's birth. Having had a child with special needs themselves, they understood and stayed close to us all of David's life.

Our world had now become so small. We were thankful for comforting, helpful friends as we tried to maintain some balance in life. Losing the strength to call people ourselves, we were grateful for those who contacted us, making deliberate efforts to support and surround us.

December 12

We were able, with a lot of effort, to get David to church this morning. We sat in the back on a padded bench, so David could lie down and stretch out. As the service was ending, Harry got up with David and began to walk toward the exit. Suddenly our pastor called out, "Wait, everyone, is David Knol still here?"

"YES, I AM!" David yelled, as he hung onto Harry.

"Well," Jack said, "David Knol is going to have a birthday on Tuesday. He is going to be twenty-two years old. I was thinking, David, since most of us will not be able to see you on Tuesday, is it okay if we sing to you today?"

"YEAH, SURE, GO AHEAD!" David yelled. His head swinging from side to side, David grinned and listened as the congregation sang happy birthday. When the song ended, David started clapping and everyone joined him in a round of applause.

There I sat, sobbing, overwhelmed with sorrow and love.

Tuesday, December 14, 2004 — David's twenty-second birthday

Early in the morning, David called out from his bed, "Hi, Mom, is it my birthday?" And so began the day. He wanted to open gifts immediately. We gave him a few to unwrap, but his main objective had been to receive a bowling set. "No, I need a bowling ball and bowling pins!" he complained, tossing aside the other gifts. Rachel wasn't planning to give him this gift until evening, so we called her at school and let her know there was a little problem brewing at home. She saved the day by letting David open his Silly Six Pins game right away.

Later Harry met the two of us at David's school, where we delivered cupcakes and noisemakers to his class. The party horns were a huge hit, with David proud and pleased.

David's birthday order was lunch at Burger King followed by a pizza supper at home with relatives.

The Friendship Class Christmas program was also that evening. The day was probably too busy, but David wanted to go. Very aware that this birthday was one we hadn't expected to celebrate, we took in every moment and filled the entire day. David loved it all.

Mid-December

The hospice chaplain came by the next day with a balloon for David's birthday. I cautioned her that David had a history of talking about balloons but being afraid to have one near him; however, this one he fell in love with. A new obsession developed. Rarely did he let it leave his side; he slept with it, patted it, talked to it, and hugged it.

David had always been fascinated with balloon talk, and his favorite books all contained a balloon reference: *Goodnight Moon, The Magic Blanket,* and *Winnie the Pooh and the Honey Tree.* Diane brought over a new book for David called *Curious George and the Hot Air Balloon,* which became a new favorite.

Once Jared and Rachel returned home for Christmas break, the house bustled with activity. With David relatively stable, Harry, Jared, Rachel, John, and I went skiing at a northern Michigan resort a few hours away. Harry's parents moved into our house to care for David while we were away for a few days. No problems arose, and they had a wonderful time together. They were good sports about listening to David's choice of loud music, usually Eric Clapton. Although it was difficult to leave David, we knew that he was in good hands and his grandparents would call immediately with any concerns. We all enjoyed ourselves.

Christmas Eve

We opened gifts, and for David the highlight was a new helium balloon from Rachel. "My buddy red balloon!" he called out. And so red it became, even though to our eyes it was blue.

At 11:00 p.m. we attended the Christmas Eve candlelight service at our church. Thankful to be there together, I tried to press every detail into memory. Near the end of the service, the congregation filed forward to receive communion, then took candles and formed a large circle around the perimeter of the worship space. The lights were dimmed. We found a chair so David could sit beside us while we stood singing "Silent Night." My body tense with sadness and love, I sensed God's peace and love surrounding and upholding us.

Christmas Day

We enjoyed a quiet day at home together. At times David would lie awake in bed, quiet and still. At other times he'd have spurts of energy and call out, "Jared, I want to FIGHT!"

In the evening, Rachel and I read him the book *Someday Heaven,* a recent birthday gift from my brother Charlie and his family. Quickly it had become a favorite because it spoke of Jesus going up to heaven like a balloon. Tonight David's enthusiastic response was, "Just like I will go to heaven like a balloon. I think I'll go tomorrow like a balloon to heaven."

December 30

At an appointment with Dr. Smith. David's blood pressure was extremely high. Dr. Smith prescribed a medication that, he explained, would contribute to further kidney damage but was needed to avoid a stroke, seizures, or other complications of high blood pressure.

Dr. Smith was pleased that David had enjoyed celebrating his twenty-second birthday and Christmas. We reviewed David's varied energy levels and reported a decrease in complaints of nausea and tingling/aching feet, with the medications Dr. Smith had ordered. His calcium levels remained good; eye drops helped his infrequent eye discomfort.

But David's nighttime breathing remained labored. He seemed to sleep despite this difficulty, but the sound kept Harry and me on alert most nights, his bedroom being next to ours.

Preparing to enter a new year, I wondered what lay ahead.

Photo by Jeff Dykehouse

letting go

January 2005

On New Year's Day we took a drive up to the cottage. Harry bundled David up and gave him a fast sled ride over the frozen lake, with David laughing and bouncing in delight.

David's school day became shorter, as I let him rest longer in the mornings. After school he would generally sleep for the rest of the afternoon. One afternoon he began a new routine — every five to ten minutes he would walk to the bathroom to get a drink or run cool water over his hands. As I watched him at the sink with water running through his fingers, I asked what he was doing. He turned off the faucet and did not reply, seemingly unsure. The cool water must have just felt good. We reminded ourselves that there was more going on inside his body than he could understand or put into words.

David frequently talked about finding a river. At this time of year it was harder to get near running water, but I found a park alongside the nearby Thornapple River where I could park close to the water. Several times we drove there and sat with our windows down — in fifteen-degree weather — listening to the roaring river and talking about the water.

David still insisted on going to Friendship Class most Tuesday evenings. Although he wanted to do his favorite things, we realized we needed to choose carefully how he spent his energy. It was a constant balancing act.

As January wore on, David was staying home from school more often. On one of these mornings his teacher called. "The class is heading to Chuck E. Cheese's for lunch to celebrate a birthday," she said. "Can you and David join us?" David was all for the idea — he had loved that place for years. So we went, and he ate several slices of pizza and insisted on cramming himself into many of the little rides.

From there we drove to an appointment with Joel, David's longtime barber. Getting a haircut was big on David's social calendar, and Joel always enjoyed David and was very patient with him. We had been told that a side effect of the new anti-hypertensive medication was thicker, faster-growing hair, and that certainly proved to be true. Much to David's delight, we began scheduling his haircuts every two weeks. Neither of us minded the long drive, as it gave us something to do; plus, car rides had become soothing to him — and to me too.

I thought about something a friend, herself an RN, had asked me: "Is it easier or harder to be a nurse during this process?" Without question, I was thankful to have an understanding of what was going on and to have insight into what was best for David. And while this process might have been easier for me as a mother had I been a little less aware, yet I knew that without insight and understanding I would have had greater frustration and possibly less peace.

Recalling our frustration and lack of understanding during David's NICU experience made us thankful that we were more knowledgeable now, able to participate in decision-making and care. In addition, several good friends who happened to be nurses chose to stay close to us, available to discuss monitoring David at home. Since I wasn't always able to remain objective as an RN anymore, these friends helped us see things more clearly.

Twenty-two years ago we had no idea what we were getting into. Neither did we realize how much David needed to teach us and how marvelously God would supply people, strength, and grace to help us along the way.

Continued support

Friends came for dinner one Sunday noon. Now living a few hours away, they had been keeping close track of how David and we were doing. David, sitting at the table with us eating mashed potatoes, asked, "Where's the sprouts?" Brussels sprouts happened to be his and Harry's favorite vegetable to eat with mashed potatoes, but I had learned not to expect others to respond quite so favorably to them. So at this meal we had corn, which David made clear was a big disappointment!

Later that day we went to Diane's for pizza, a common Sunday-evening routine. David happily lounged on the sofa, flicking their wire whisk.

Sandy called one evening, knowing how fragile we were becoming. It helped us tremendously to share concerns, fears, and grief with those who were brave enough to ask. Many people knew that David was not well but did not grasp just how serious and draining the atmosphere at our house had become.

This group of friends and family became our lifeline of support and encouragement. We felt isolated, alone, and scared. Their calls, visits, and e-mails allowed me to connect by filling them in on David's status — and by finding out what was happening in their own lives, if I had the energy to ask.

Life is so busy for people, I reflected — too busy. I told myself I'd need to remember to control my busyness and keep a proper balance when I returned to normal life.

The spiritual dimensions of water

A new hospice nurse came by this month. I was disappointed that this nurse was so young and inexperienced. What I really hoped for was someone who would support and take care of us as we managed David. I probably was not the easiest parent to satisfy, so I tried to be mindful of behaving appropriately myself.

Rachel dropped in almost every day now, which David loved. With Valentine's Day approaching, she decided to help David get his Valentine cards ready for his friends at school. Rachel, following their routine, asked David to name his classmates. One by one, he remembered each of them.

Having people come and go helped alleviate our isolation and provided stimulation and entertainment for David. Jared, too, was working hard to stay involved and be a part of what was going on at home, calling often.

One night David had a rough time. The next morning he was eager to return to the Thornapple River. His increasing urge to hear water fascinated us. My friend Sharon, a pastor, pointed out the spiritual dimensions of water, making us wonder anew at David's instincts and to recommit ourselves to letting him lead us.

Bowling still sounded good to David, so one afternoon in late January, Harry and some friends took him to the lanes. He helped bowl and enjoyed all the activity, but after one game, it was clear that he needed to return home. He slept the rest of the afternoon. That evening Rachel and John came over, as well as other friends.

David was now asking for two baths a day and staying in the tub for a long soak each time.

Diane and her family came over for pizza another night and brought a green balloon for David. I now kept bags of balloons in the house, since David asked for several throughout the day, liking them only as long as they felt firm. Red balloons were everywhere, floating out of his room into other parts of the house.

January 31

At 5:30 a.m. David called out, asking for a bath. As I helped him into the tub, I noted increased swelling throughout his body. Afterwards I weighed him and found he was ninety-one pounds, up eight to ten pounds since the new anti-hypertensive medication began. I wondered how much this was contributing to the swelling. With his blood pressure not dropping even with increased doses, I also wondered whether we should back off on this medication.

Sandy came in the morning to help. She went with David and me to Dr. Thomas's office to discuss David's symptoms and complaints. I let the staff know we were on our way. "Would you be able to let us in through the back door so we can go directly to an exam room?" I asked. I was finished with waiting rooms.

Before arriving, I also told Dr. Smith's office about my concerns. I had been advised to call Dr. Smith for any kidney-related trouble and Dr. Thomas for other complaints — but I wasn't sure any longer whom to call for what. The two doctors talked by phone while we were in the office, trying to determine the situation and what to do about it. Carefully

Dr. Thomas said to me, "Faye, you're swimming upstream, you know." Yes, I knew. But we still had symptoms to treat.

I asked both doctors if the new medication should be decreased or even stopped, since it seemed to be bringing on more problems. Both doctors said we needed to keep David on it, that we could only hope it was doing some good. Running such high blood pressures, he was at great risk for a stroke or seizures, and we had to know we had done everything possible to prevent those complications.

Both doctors noted David's decline and asked how hospice was supporting us. Recognizing the additional support we would need to continue caring for David at home, they gave me their private phone and pager numbers, insisting I call with any questions or concerns.

February 4

David's face looked slightly less swollen today, although it seemed worse in the morning, after he had been lying flat all night. We tried to elevate his head, but he quickly threw the extra pillows on the floor.

Dan and Sandy stopped by early in the evening, and other friends came to check on us later David still loved visitors and continued to do better when we had plans and guests. Every day he wanted to invite someone over, and if I couldn't reach the first person he suggested, he would rattle off names of others to call. He didn't understand that not everyone could come at a moment's notice. Plus, calling people was taking more energy than I could muster.

February 5

Harry took David to Home Depot today. Riding in a cart was always great fun for him. The two of them had done this together for years, David always a great companion.

On weekdays David had always been the best thing for Harry to come home from work to. The minute Harry entered the house David would call to him, ready to wrestle, and Harry could release all the stress of his workday playing with David. Over the past few months, Jared and Rachel had both expressed concern over what David's loss would mean to Harry in this respect.

We had each claimed bits of David and made them part of who we ourselves were and how we functioned. Our minds could not grasp the loss we faced.

February 6

Harry went to church this morning and asked for prayers on David's behalf — comfort for David and strength for us all. This was the first public announcement of David's illness. It was time. Many people had been aware and praying for him all along, but we had continued to refrain from public announcements to avoid the possibility that someone might question or challenge our decision not to pursue dialysis and transplant. The difficult and controversial case of Terri Schiavo was then much in the national news.

My nephew Andrew came for lunch. From California, he was at a college near our home. We had enjoyed getting to know him better this year and appreciated his involvement in our lives. David loved getting to know his cousin, and Andrew figured out quickly how to have fun with David.

Though David had been quiet during the meal, he announced afterward, "I want to go to the beach and feel the sand. How about we go?" So Harry, David, and I took off for Lake Michigan. He was very happy in the car, bouncing and talking most of the way. The closer we got to the beach, however, the quieter he became. As we parked the car he asked, "Mom, do we have a blanket?" Harry carried him, wrapped in the blanket, to a bench along the channel, where he wanted to lie down on my lap.

It was mild outside as we sat together, felt the sand, and listened to the wind, waves, and seagulls. After about three minutes David quietly said, "I need to go home now." Harry carried David back to the car, where he slept, his breathing labored, as we drove home.

Back at home, David asked for a Rice Krispie bar. He ate one after another until he'd devoured all eight in the package. As good a meal as any, I figured.

Harry's brothers and their families came late in the afternoon. In the evening I talked on the phone to Jared, who was calling daily to get updates and talk to David.

February 8

Rachel dropped a class, lightening her load so she could come home more often. Diane called to invite David to spend the afternoon at her house, asking Harry and me to come for supper later. "No," yelled David, "I'll just go — you and Dad have to go somewhere!" David sat up in bed and waited until Diane came to get him.

Harry and I went out and did some shopping. We picked up a bag of shredded bark because David had been asking for woodchips. When we returned home, Harry poured out a pile on the kitchen floor. David was elated, fully aware of how silly and unusual this was. "I'm sitting on the pile, Mom," he said, laughing in delight.

Harry's co-workers gave us an "encouragement tree" — an ivy plant decked with gift cards and certificates for movies, stores, restaurants, a pedicure, and a massage, along with lotions, slippers, cookie cutters, and kitchen towels. The attached card said that while they were able to keep Harry busy at work, their arms couldn't stretch long enough to reach me, so this was their way of offering me support. What amazingly kind and thoughtful people — and most of them I had never met.

February 9

At 1:30 a.m. David called out calmly, asking me to lie in bed with him. He complained of a sore throat. Then he talked about woodchips and asked how long it would be till May, when new woodchips would be spread outside. "I wish it was May now," he said quietly. I could not bear to think ahead to May.

Sheri came to help in the morning, and we decided it was a good day to deliver David's Valentine's Day cards to his friends at school. We went, and David was delighted to hear their voices — it had been a while since he had made it to school. Having insisted on bringing a red balloon, he hung onto it as he sat at the table across from Joey, his best friend in class. The two of them talked, laughed, and played catch with the balloon, having a grand time. How quickly this tired David, though.

David asked Sheri to join us on our daily drive to the river, after which she offered to watch David for a few hours, at our house or hers. "Your house," David insisted, still wanting to socialize.

Our pastor came later in the afternoon. David was agitated. Jack gently asked me if I thought we would be able to continue keeping David home, given how involved his care was becoming. Keeping David home had been our goal, but I was beginning to realize we might need to consider in-patient hospice care soon.

February 10

At 3:00 a.m. David wanted ice cream and then asked me to lie with him and hold onto his throat.

In the morning I updated the doctors on the changes we were seeing. A bit later Harry's parents came so I could go out to get my hair trimmed. They planned to drive David to the river and then get him some french fries. I felt anxious about going — it was getting harder to leave David even briefly. After my hair appointment, I did some shopping, arriving home by mid-afternoon. Harry's parents told me that they had read books to David until about 10:30 a.m. but that he had been sleeping ever since and they'd been unable to rouse him. Rachel had stopped home while I was away and even she had been unable to wake him.

Immediately I walked into his room, helped him out of bed, and encouraged him to eat and drink. I was bothered that he'd been down for so many hours. Gradually, though, I realized that I might have to get used to the idea of his sleeping more and shouldn't necessarily force him awake. He seemed to know what he needed.

When Harry returned home from work, I told him how bad I felt that David had slept a good part of the day. Harry gently responded, "Well, Faye, maybe it's a good thing you were gone awhile so you didn't have to feel bad all day."

The three of us drove to the Thornapple and listened to the water. Diane stopped by later and read books to David. In the evening other friends came over, but David fell asleep early.

February 11

Around 4:00 a.m. David asked for some tea with honey, which seemed to soothe his throat. He went back to sleep, then awoke early, eager to go have his blood drawn. Our friend Karen came early in the morning, gave David his bath, and went with us to the lab. Our regular lab tech was there, much to David's delight; she made sure he achieved his goal of a Garfield Band-Aid.

Afterward David and I returned to the river. An important part of this routine was traveling a stretch of M-6 to get there — he always checked to make sure I was planning to take the highway so we could go fast while he bounced in the backseat.

Diane brought over a cassette tape of hot air balloon stories that her daughter had written and recorded for David. He loved it. After sleeping part of the evening, he got up and ate two bags of popcorn, then wanted a bath. In the tub he started to obsess about wanting a life jacket; I noticed slight confusion in his language.

February 12

Rachel came over to help for the day. We decided David could use a haircut so I called Joel to make an appointment for later that morning. Because his hair needed washing, I wanted David to have a bath prior to going, but he was hypersensitive to the water and would not get in. Gradually Rachel coaxed him into the tub as she read a book to distract him.

Once Joel helped David settle into his familiar haircut routine, he finally relaxed.

February 13

David and Harry played a lot of Silly Six Pins today, and the entertainment continued when Rachel came home for dinner with three of her friends.

Valentine's Day

At about 4:00 a.m. David called out, "Happy Valentine's Day, Mom!" David *loved* holidays and their predictable routines.

Harry and I helped him take his medications and drink an instant breakfast before he went back to sleep. It was difficult for me to see him sleep so much. I had always been responsible for this guy, and now his care was more than I could fully understand.

A more experienced hospice RN arrived in the afternoon. She immediately ordered a hospital bed for

David to get his head elevated, which would help his breathing.

Thoughtful friends brought over a delicious Valentine's Day dinner for us to enjoy. That evening David fretted over the idea that a hospital bed would be delivered tomorrow. "Do I need a hospital gown? Will I need anesthesia?" he asked, remembering his last outpatient experience years ago, when he received tubes in his ears.

February 15

A new hospice nurse manager, Anna, arrived at 9:00 a.m. Calmly and professionally she approached David, who was sitting in the beanbag chair in his bedroom, and introduced herself. She sat on the floor next to him and answered all of his questions about who she was. I was relieved to see the comfort she so quickly exhibited with David. He had been up since 6:00 a.m., anxious, waiting for the hospital bed to arrive.

Anna observed widespread swelling in David and explained that she had worked with dialysis patients for many years before moving to hospice care. She expressed respect for the decision we'd made to pursue comfort and quality-of-life care for David, describing times when people brought confused, elderly family members for dialysis, and how horrible it was for the individual *and* for the staff. In those cases, when the patient didn't understand what was going on, she said the nurses would often ask the doctor whether someone had forgotten to share with the family the valid option of palliative care.

When the hospital bed arrived, the hospice nurse was still there. I needed to move David from his room so the deliverymen could set the bed up, but I'd forgotten to anticipate David's heightened anxiety. He couldn't understand what this new bed would mean for him, and it was a struggle for me to move him — David kicked, scratched, and bit me. Anna, witnessing this, quickly asked whether I needed her help. When I said no, she remained calm and steady. What an introduction to David — I was thankful it didn't seem to rattle her.

Once the hospital bed was set up, Anna helped me make the bed with David's flannel sheets and comforter. I helped him into bed, where he calmed down and began to relax in his familiar bedding. The controls for the bed were within his reach, but he didn't seem to notice or care when we put the bed up and down. *How strange,* I thought. David, who was so in tune to his environment, was not reacting to the motion of this bed. He recognized his sheets and comforter, and that was all he cared about.

Later the hospice chaplain stopped by. She was kind, calm, and spiritually focused, and I appreciated talking with her.

David was sleepy throughout the day and asked for three baths. Sheri and Randy called to ask whether they could come over in the evening. Their kindness and support helped us immensely, allowing us to review the day's events together.

February 16

At 9:00 a.m. a new hospice social worker arrived. She sat on the floor next to David's beanbag chair and talked with him about books, balloons, trucks, rivers, and car washes. He was delighted to meet her and discuss some of his favorite topics.

She also spent time talking with me and assessing how I was doing. Studying me, she said, "You have no energy to spare, Faye. I hope you realize this. You need to eliminate any people in your life who *drain from you* and only allow near you those who build you up and are helpful." We had already come to realize that it was only those people who were now bravely walking right with us, helping and supporting us, who could even bear to be near us and our pain.

The hospice home health aide came by mid-day and read books to David.

Andrew came over and spent time with me in the afternoon while David slept. His presence was comforting as he sat with me, keeping me company and conversing. Simply being present and chatting helped steady me. When David woke up, Andrew joined us on our drive to the Thornapple.

February 17

At 3:00 a.m. David asked for a bath. I read to him, able to hold off the bath until 5:00 a.m.

To our delight, our close friend Mary came over in the morning with her son. Next came Rachel. The comfort and strength Mary's presence provided were just what Rachel and I needed; we wept while Mary prayed with us at David's bedside. Mary also went to the grocery store to pick up a few items for us, including a box of Life cereal, David's latest obsession. I hadn't bought that cereal in years, but in the past week he'd decided he needed a lot of it.

We were now talking to Jared several times a day. He made plans to fly home on the 26th for his spring break, following midterm exams.

February 18

David began calling out at about 1:30 a.m. with complaints of a sore throat. He asked me to lie beside him, and I sang to him and massaged his back.

Harry and I had been talking about how God was providing an extra measure of patience, strength, and grace. It was becoming increasingly difficult for Harry to go to work, but it was hard to know whether he should start staying home more — we just couldn't predict how long this phase would last. We had gotten so used to pacing ourselves over the past year, and it was still hard to know what to anticipate. The hospice staff and doctors could not predict either.

After lunch the hospice home health aide came by to spend time with David. David asked for multiple balloons. Calmly and cheerfully, she started blowing up balloons and tying them together, creating what she called the "balloon cluster game," much to David's delight. He liked those words.

Diane dropped in, knowing that with a hospice aide caring for David, I could step out. Then Janice came from church, and Diane offered to stay in the house and do some cleaning while I went for a walk with Janice. Diane loved that if she stayed nearby, I would be comfortable to leave David briefly. The day was becoming too busy, but I needed to see these people. As we walked in the neighborhood, I talked with Janice about how our church handled memorial services, food, etc., as the reality of losing David was getting closer.

Exhausted as I was, my mind still was racing, trying to keep track of everything I thought I should be thinking of. Comfort came in checking off details. By the time I returned, the home health aide had left and Diane had gotten David into the bathtub.

Later another friend stopped by, bringing us a collection of restaurant gift cards and take-out menus. This was a most welcome gift, as it was hard to think about cooking — calling ahead for take-out would be so helpful.

I called Dr. Smith's office and the hospice nurse to discuss David's increased agitation and nighttime restlessness. After getting a new medication order from Dr. Smith, a hospice nurse came right over with it. She explained the drug carefully to Harry and me, and we gave him an initial dose. It was just after 5:00 p.m.

The nurse looked at me then and said, "Faye, you need to go to bed *right now.*" I did, and Harry took over, thanking this hospice nurse, with tears in his eyes, for the support and the sense of trust and security she and her colleagues were giving us.

A couple of hours later, I got up to find that Harry had prepared a wonderful dinner for the two of us and our friends Dave and Karen, who had asked to come over. Noticing a significant decline in David, Dave tried a "kaboom" with him. David did not respond. They wept with us.

February 19

Harry got up with David a few times during the night but was able to settle him down quickly each time, so we both awoke this Saturday feeling surprisingly refreshed. We were trying to grab moments of rest whenever we could, amazed at how little sleep we could function on.

David was not eating or drinking much at all. Yet he was so pleased to have Harry home and kept wanting to wrestle: "What kind of fight shall we do, Dad, a bee-sting fight?" He ate a few bites of food as the day went on. He did not want a bath.

Harry, David, and I drove to the river together.

Later Rachel came home and said she would stay and help with David during the night so Harry and I could get some sleep. As painful as it was for her to come home, we were grateful for her presence. Rachel had a close friend who had lost her mother years earlier. This friend had advised Rachel early on in David's illness that no matter how difficult it became, she needed to keep coming home and stay involved with her brother.

February 20

Rachel and I got up together to care for David several times during the night when he called out. Often we found him lying quietly in bed just flicking his spatula.

Harry and I went to church in the morning while Rachel stayed with David. It was good to be strengthened there this day.

David's teacher, Cheryl, and her husband came over in the afternoon. David's response to Cheryl was beautiful, a delight for us all to see. The moment he heard her voice, he sat up in bed with a huge smile, then grabbed her hand and brought it to his cheek, sniffing and kissing it to show his great love for her. It was the biggest response we had seen from him in days.

David didn't want to take a drive today, nor did he want to sit in his beanbag chair. Most of the day, he slept. We thought we would skip going to Diane's for pizza tonight, but David was determined that we should go.

At Diane's David refused to eat but was happy to lie on the sofa, flicking her whisk. We stayed for about an hour and then returned home, with David pleased and satisfied.

Soon John called to ask, "Could Dave and I stop by yet tonight?" We knew Dave well, and David was happy to talk with both of them from his bed. When they were done visiting with David, the two young men sat at the kitchen table with me for over an hour. We discussed living and dying and knowing God's presence. I was deeply moved to be able to answer their insightful questions, sharing thoughts and feelings with them.

Before going to bed, I thought about all of the changes taking place and decided I should take David's blood pressure before giving his blood-pressure medication. Since he'd taken only sips of liquid and a few bites of food over the past two days, I thought his blood pressure might be dropping. At 10:00 p.m. it was 180/120 — extremely elevated.

Monday, February 21

Harry and I were each up several times with David during the night. Things were changing quickly. Catching bits of rest whenever we could, we found it hard to see things clearly.

Around 5:30 a.m. David woke up again and called, "Dad, come fight me! Let's wrestle!" When Harry got to his room, David asked, "Dad, what are we going to do tonight? Go sledding!" Harry had planned to stay home from work, but seeing David so full of energy, we commented that perhaps it was going to be a better day and decided together that Harry should go to work for a few hours.

The hospice social worker came mid-morning and read books to David. Although he was polite to her, he insisted on staying in bed. He appeared to be sleeping, but as soon as she finished one book, he would ask for another one by name.

It had been more than two days since he'd had his hair washed, and seeing it limp bothered me. After the social worker left, I was able to talk David into taking a quick bath. I washed his hair as quickly as possible and noticed he seemed confused. Helping him out of the tub, I gently rubbed lotion onto his body and helped him into his favorite gray sweatpants and red sweatshirt, just out of the dryer. We walked back to his bedroom together. *That's better,* I thought, *he looks clean and fresh.* And David was satisfied to have on his favorite clothing.

After getting David settled, I called Anna and Harry, making them aware of the changes I was seeing. Anna said she would be right over. Harry said he would come too, but then we decided to wait and see what Anna thought when she assessed David. We agreed that I would let him know as soon as I had more information, and that, in any case, he would come home right after the meeting he was in had ended.

We were still pacing ourselves in response to the events in front of us. After years of training in not overreacting with this son, we could not see clearly the point to which he had come.

Anna arrived around noon. "Harry, Rachel, and Jared should come home," she gently told me. *Oh my,* I thought. *It's time. Never ready.* I called Harry, who left work immediately. I left a message for Rachel on her cell phone, knowing she was in class. Jared was in the middle of a midterm exam in Nashville. With Jared in midterms all week and scheduled to fly home on Saturday, I hoped that David could hold on until then.

Harry arrived soon after Anna had left and rushed to David's room, instantly seeing the change in him since morning. Soon a friend arrived with lunch, which I gratefully accepted at the door, explaining I could no longer spend time with her as planned. She graciously understood. As Harry and I quickly ate this meal, we realized the timing of her arrival was perfect, since we wouldn't otherwise have thought of eating.

Rachel's roommate answered Rachel's cell phone, having noticed my frequent attempts to reach her. She knew which lab Rachel was in and offered to run and get her out of class. Rachel arrived home by 1:55 p.m.

David kept requesting his favorite books by name, but as we would start reading he would lose focus and ask for another book.

The hospice chaplain called and said she would update our church staff. I was aware that our pastor had just returned to town following the death of his mother out of state. Relieved that he was back, I also felt sadness for his loss in the midst of the critical state we were in. The hospice social worker called to offer help with phone calls or anything else we needed.

Sandy telephoned and, hearing Rachel answer the phone, asked, "What is going on?" When Rachel told her, she offered to come right over with her husband, Dan. Harry, Rachel, and I agreed their presence would be helpful.

By mid-afternoon I was able to get in touch with Jared, who had just finished his first test of the week. "You need to come home, Jared," I simply stated. He paused, asked for details, and said, "I'll work on getting there as soon as possible." Anna had supplied information on how to make his flight a priority with the airlines.

At around 3:30 David asked, "Can you read *The Christmas Story*?" Dan and Sandy arrived, calm and steady. As Dan spoke, David weakly said, "No kabooms, Dan."

Jared called to say he was having trouble with flights but was working with the airlines. We placed the phone by David's ear. As Jared told David he loved him and was coming home soon, David weakly whispered, "I love you, Jared." Minutes later, shortly before 5:00 pm, David appeared to sleep.

As we made phone calls to our closest friends and family, many of them asked whether they could come to the house.

Dr. Smith called to check on us and gave instructions for additional relief if David's restlessness should reappear.

Our church household group, who had been alerted to the situation, met in another home, with other church members joining them in prayer for us.

Sandy realized we should contact Dr. Thomas, so she called him with an update. He asked to talk to me, saying, "If David should pass away during the night, I want to be called so I can come right over, and otherwise I will stop by late tomorrow morning."

We stayed right by David's side, stroking, singing, and talking to him. Friends gathered in our kitchen, sharing their David stories, and took turns staying at his bedside to support us. A few times they all gathered in David's room as we sang his favorite songs, read a comforting psalm, and prayed together. People brought food to the house and friends encouraged me to eat, but I declined. My stomach was in such knots that I felt it would probably be harmful for me to eat. I just kept drinking water and hot tea.

I kept waiting for David to wake up, asking repeatedly, "David, what is going on?" David, who always had something to say, was silent.

So we simply talked to him and assured him of our presence and love.

Three of Rachel's friends came to the house, delivering her personal items from the dorm. They stayed with us for some time, supporting Rachel and joining us beside David.

By 11:00 p.m. Jared arrived home. Gratefully we embraced him, our circle of care for David now complete.

Though David remained unresponsive all night as family members stayed beside him, we were aware that David's senses could still be functioning. Earlier in the evening several had witnessed Harry's letting go of David's hand as he got up to get something to drink and David appearing to reach out towards Harry's hand.

Tuesday, February 22, 2005 — David's final day

Anna returned at 7:30 a.m., saying it was hard to know how long David's young heart would sustain him.

As she left, several close friends began arriving. When Sharon came, I asked her to be in charge. She became our gatekeeper that day, calmly and efficiently keeping things running during this highly emotional time. We were overwhelmed with gratitude that these people were willing to share this time with us — and we actually surprised ourselves that we were willing to allow it. But we had needed to share David's care throughout the years, and these friends had invested themselves in our family. Now they weren't letting go of us — nor we of them.

In the end, we found we needed the help of friends and family during those last two days to be able to release David. It was more than we could do alone. These people bravely entered and shared this holy time with us. On Monday evening and throughout Tuesday, Harry and I felt a greater presence within our home, the presence of angels in various forms surrounding us.

Dr. Thomas arrived in the late morning and spent more than an hour beside David with the four of us. He prayed with us and reflected on the remarkable person David was, and on how much he and all of us had learned from him.

At 12:45 p.m. my mom and sister arrived from California. My dad, not able to travel, telephoned a half-hour later, asking for an update. "Is David able to understand if I could talk to him on the phone?" he asked. We weren't sure, Harry said, but it was possible. "How about you do the routine you always do with David on the phone?" As we held the telephone by David's ear, my eighty-three-year-old father crowed like a rooster, yodeled, and then sang a silly song David loved (something David always insisted he do). Smiles of delight passed over our faces as we listened.

At 1:30 p.m. the spirit of our precious son and brother — and friend — was gently lifted from our arms.

For the next three hours, we stayed by his bedside, with family, friends, and our pastor surrounding and upholding us. Only gradually could we grasp without a shadow of a doubt that the life within his body had gone. As I sat on a chair beside David, holding onto him, I could feel friends taking turns slipping into the chair with me, holding onto me.

His life was complete. Our goal of allowing him to live as comfortably and as happily as we possibly could was attained.

Our loss was overwhelming.

The next day, Jared sat down at the computer and composed his brother's obituary for the newspaper:

> David Harry Knol began his life on December 14, 1982, and was gently lifted into the arms of his Savior on February 22, 2005. Born prematurely,

David was not expected to live more than a few hours but instead grew to be a confident, happy, and opinionated young man. David loved life, and his contagious joy, unique sense of humor, and boundless curiosity enriched the lives of all who came to know him. The memory of his life will always be a source of joy and inspiration for his parents, brother, sister, grandparents, and many aunts, uncles, and cousins. He will also be remembered by his longtime teacher, Cheryl, the staff and students of Lincoln School, and the numerous friends who enriched his life by generously welcoming him into their own. The family would like to express gratitude for the expert and compassionate care provided by Dr. [Thomas] and Dr. [Smith].

During the week hundreds of people filed through at the funeral home visitations. Friends, relatives, co-workers, nurses, doctors, teachers, and bus drivers all waited for a chance to speak with us. Some we hadn't seen in years, yet they came to honor David. Red balloons and pineapples were included in several of the flower arrangements people sent.

As I acknowledged the loss, my eyes frequently darted to my son's open casket. Our pastor had advised, "Your eyes will need to see what your mind cannot grasp." This proved true for me. How could he be so still? Over and over again my mind worked on that concept, then and for a long time after.

In the months leading up to his death, Rachel had created an electronic slideshow of David's life. Shown during the memorial service, this presentation was a vibrant portrayal of the active, joyful life David lived. Our pastor led the service, with Dr. Thomas and our friend Randy offering memories, observations, stories, and insights about David. We sang the hymns "Be Thou My Vision" and "My Jesus, I Love Thee." The service ended with the "Romans Doxology," another song David loved. He had always softly echoed the last Amens after everyone else had finished. That day his *Amen* seemed to fill the air around me.

Cards and letters arrived by the hundreds in the following weeks. We read and reread each one. Profound words of love and memories of David were shared. One person wrote, "I will pray as you first recuperate and then redefine your lives." Those words spoke exactly of the state we were in — exhausted, lost, and empty. David united us. In his loss we clung to each other.

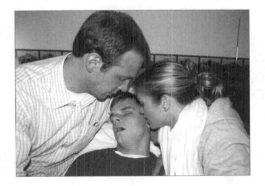

redefining and remembering

The early months

Weeks after we lost David, our friend Al said he had something to share with us. On the night of February 21, he told us, he had gone to bed knowing David was unresponsive. He awoke during the night and heard the words, "Pray for Harry and Faye." Al thought, *No, shouldn't I be praying for David?* He then heard, "I have David taken care of — David is okay. Pray for Harry and Faye."

Al said he began praying for us, dozed off, then awoke to find the scenario repeating itself. So he pressed on, offering specific prayers for us throughout David's last night.

We had held out hope during his last twenty hours that David would awaken one more time and talk to us. This did not happen. After wondering whether he had suffered during that time, God's spirit spoke to us through a friend.

———

In the first month after losing David, I lost weight. This puzzled me, but then I realized that throughout David's life I had been taking bites while feeding him, before or after my own meal. Gradually I came to understand that our lifestyle, including our eating habits, was changing in David's absence. I was struck by how physical grief was. I was rarely hungry and had to remind myself to eat.

———

Harry and I chose a marker for David's grave. Under his name we listed the dates of his birth and death and then simply the word *Beloved*, which had been the title of the message our pastor had given at David's memorial service.

The next months brought mixed emotions and struggle. I wasn't sure I wanted to work as an RN any longer. Empty, I couldn't generate the strength to care for anyone. My employer was understanding and patient, allowing me the time I needed.

Our son's life, we felt, had been complete. And yet we grieved — not only the loss of him, but the loss of the role he played in our family. Some thought that after arranging our lives around David's needs for twenty-two years, we would now have a sense of relief. No one said this to us directly, but we knew that family and friends were hearing such comments. Employment, marriage, and children were not in David's future; his needs would have been continuous and demanding. But we had loved him. And now there is always someone — and a piece of our own life — missing. There's a massive hole in our hearts, a void in our lives.

A change of space

Even while David was still living, we had thought about moving from our home of nineteen years. We had chosen the area of town where we wanted to relocate but kept pushing the idea aside as David's illness progressed. Now Harry felt it was time. I didn't think this was a good idea. Wasn't it always said that people should avoid making big life changes in the first year of loss?

But by early May 2005 our building plans were settled and our house was for sale. I felt somewhat dragged into the project, led by Harry and urged along by Rachel and Jared, who fully supported the idea. As our plans developed, I came to understand that this project was temporarily filling part of the hole in my life — I became preoccupied with the planning of our new home.

Creating a new place of comfort and refuge became our goal. A friend warned us that for good and for bad, we were delaying some of our grief by immersing ourselves in such a big project. We were aware.

A few people thought we wanted to move so quickly because David had died in our home. That was not so. All four of us were at peace with the fact that his dying had occurred in the place where he was most comfortable.

In mid-June, while we were visiting with our friends Dan and Sandy, their daughter Stephanie asked me, "Faye, have you started cleaning out David's room?"

"No," I told her, "I haven't, but I probably should since our house is for sale. Is there anything of David's that you would like?" Stephanie was twenty-two years old and had been a premature baby alongside David in the NICU. She's an insightful young woman who's living with her own physical and cognitive challenges. She loves music as David had, so I asked, "Maybe some of his CDs?"

She agreed to that idea, but added, "I really liked David's Silly Six Pins." She had sat on our kitchen floor many times with David, rolling the ball into the squawking pins. The game had been David's last birthday gift from Rachel and Jared, so I told Stephanie I would have to talk to them.

The next day I looked in David's closet, found the Silly Six Pins game, and gathered some CDs for Stephanie. I noticed that my frame of mind was surprisingly calm and reflective — it probably was a good idea to keep sorting. The scent, memories, and feelings of David were distinctly present, which I welcomed, feeling comforted and amazed by them. Within a few hours, several piles had accumulated around the bedroom.

The following evening a young couple, having noticed the For Sale sign, stopped at our door and asked to see the house. The place was in disarray, and David's room still had piles of stuff everywhere. Normally we wouldn't have shown the house so spontaneously, but that night we did. They ended up presenting us with an offer on the spot, and once negotiations were complete, we were required to be out of the house in two weeks.

Thanks to Stephanie, who had nudged and encouraged me, the hardest part of the moving process had already been completed. The timing of her question provided the opportunity to sort and reflect on David's room slowly, with calmness and clarity of mind, before the intense packing and moving began. An apartment became our temporary home.

We spent many days that summer at our cottage in northern Michigan, still a place where we found rest and peace.

Painful transitions

Spontaneity had never been a part of our life with David. Consistency and routine were essential. We had to prepare carefully and plan everything . . . or pay the price. Surveying the scene, planning escape routes, gauging David's frustration or anxiety, watching out for his safety — these were our survival skills, and they became second nature for us. Yet there was always a certain level of tension as we cared for him, a feeling of being on alert. Our life now is spontaneous. We live without that underlying tension. It is so different.

Although we found it difficult to be in large groups in our vulnerable state, we were drawn to our church for worship. There we would gain comfort and strength, not only from our pastor's messages, but also from the music and the people. Even today a smile, a touch of the hand, a hug, a knowing look, and acknowledging words speak to our loss and grief.

The same friends and family members who had walked closely with us throughout David's final journey continued to uphold and watch out for us in our grief. Calling and checking on us often, they would share memories and provide a listening ear, allowing us to grieve and talk about our loss. Kindness and love were just what we needed. We felt safe with them.

The overwhelming reality of David's being gone was, and remains, always present. Clinging to my faith and to my belief in life after death, I tried to find comfort in the thought of David's being in heaven, but the concept was not concrete enough for me. Consumed with David's absence, having lost my role as caregiver, I gradually came to accept that heaven is more than my mind can grasp.

In August my employer asked whether I would consider doing some flexible, part-time training for certified nurse aides working in hospice care. I agreed. Accompanying nurse aides on visits to care for those who could no longer care for themselves and helping them provide excellent care gave me great satisfaction.

By fall I also began subbing occasionally for the nurses on the campus of David's former school. There I was reminded that though we miss David tremendously, we no longer worry about him.

A place of refuge

In September we moved into our new home and immediately found it to be the place of comfort and refuge we had hoped it would be. Many asked us how it was possible to leave so quickly the home where our memories of David were. It surprised us too, but we felt comfortable about the move and believed that the timing was right. Though we didn't understand it at the time, by October Harry was able to identify what had pressed him so urgently into the move: "In the other house I could not stop looking for David, and it was driving me crazy. In this home I no longer look for him, but I feel his presence and am comforted."

Reminders of David are scattered throughout our new home, including several gifts from friends in the form of a pineapple — a stone outside near the front door, a glass sun-catcher, a pewter tray.

Marking milestones

December was a month difficult to anticipate with David's birthday the 14th. A colleague of Harry's told us that she and her husband take a day off from work every year on the birthday and the day they lost their child.

After thinking about it, we decided to host an open house on the evening of the 14th. We titled the invitations sent to family and friends "Celebrating Life and the Goodness of Our Relationships." The evening was a wonderful time of remembering and missing David, and of giving thanks for the beauty and blessing of our relationships. In David's memory, friends gave us a large basket, full of items for David's class at Lincoln School.

Our church has a memorial table at the side of the sanctuary that may be used by anyone wishing to remember a loved one. The Sunday before David's birthday, we set it up with a few reminders of David and his life.

After David left us, I endlessly relived and reviewed every aspect of his final days, weeks, and months. My mind was absorbed with his illness and death. It was only when I was able to begin writing about his life — about the way he lived and the things we learned from him — that I was finally able to remember him when he was healthy. I began writing furiously.

On February 22, 2006, the one-year anniversary of David's death, Rachel, Harry, and I spent the day together. Launching red balloons at David's gravesite, as we had the day we buried him, we found it hard to comprehend that a year had passed. Jared called from Nashville to talk and reflect.

A week later I came down with shingles. What timing, I thought, knowing that shingles often accompanies or follows a time of stress. It was as if my body had stored up all the stress of the past years and was now forcing me to take a break.

Lincoln School used the memorial gifts received in David's name to improve the Multi-Sensory Room — a room that David loved — with equipment designed for the visually impaired. Cheryl spearheaded the effort and involved us in choosing the equipment. By spring the additions had been installed, and a smiling photograph of David surrounded by school friends was hung at the entrance to the room. Shortly thereafter Cheryl announced her intention to retire after thirty-five years of teaching, explaining, "Several years ago I decided to keep teaching as long as David was at Lincoln School." Helping us finish the memorial project made her role there complete.

Spring

Winter turned to spring, and we watched new life emerge all around our home. At David's gravesite we placed a pineapple and some woodchips; it seemed appropriate and made us smile.

Life is taking on new meaning. We have been given a different set of eyes, and we now approach life with a view to enjoy every day and to care more deeply for those who come across our path.

Pangs

Shortly after David died, I shared with a good friend that the moment David's life ended I felt a severe physical wrenching. This deeply spiritual man reasoned that this was because David had taken a part of me with him. I was reminded of this one Sunday morning in June 2006, when we had a conversation with a man sitting near us in church. Realizing it had been over a year since we had lost David, he told us of his own experience with losing a son many years earlier. His grief had been so raw, he said, the wound so open. Time passed and the wound stayed. But, he continued, he had found that grief, though it remains, changes in character over time. We then discovered he was speaking to us on the anniversary of his son's death.

The gift of Alice

In 2000 a Grand Rapids artist had approached Lincoln School and asked to work with the visually impaired/ multiply impaired classroom on an art project called "Something Fishy." This citywide project, involving a number of schools, engaged many local artists and children in decorating large fiberglass fish sculptures, which were later displayed throughout the Grand Rapids area. We were vaguely aware that David's class was included.

In October 2006 I received a call from Jeff, the photographer who had taken pictures of our family when David was under hospice care. He told me his studio is near the studio of an artist named Reb

Roberts, who'd worked on the fish project. Reb had stopped by Jeff's studio that day and had recognized David in a photo on the wall. Learning of David's death, Reb told Jeff he wanted to meet with us.

Soon after, Reb telephoned our home, explaining that he had become very close to David during the three-week project in 2000. He had several photos of David painting, which he wanted us to have, and invited us to his studio.

When we met the following week, Reb described at length how our son had captivated him, how he'd attached himself to Reb, and how David had been the leader of the class, fully absorbed in the project. While smelling, touching, painting, and throwing glitter on the fish, David asked about the colors. He had been intrigued with color — this we knew well.

Reb went on to explain that the teacher at first had been hesitant to allow her students to be involved, thinking Reb would expect greater things from them than they could accomplish. But Reb was fascinated with the students and amazed at how interested they were in the tactile experience. Quickly he became aware of their unique perceptions and curiosity.

When the public sculpture display ended, the fish were sold — all but the one created by David's class. This fish had been stolen from its place on a street corner. About a year later it had been found and returned to Reb. He had since received many offers to purchase it but said he was unable to part with the fish because of the special memories it held. It stood in a prominent spot in his studio.

When he learned in the fall of 2006 that David had died, Reb decided that we should have the fish and was pleased that the photographer knew how to contact us. Reb gave us many pictures of himself and David painting together, photos we didn't know existed. They are a treasure. The students had named the fish, Reb noted as we left. They called it "Goodbye, Alice," he said.

That afternoon I reread a recent newspaper article featuring Reb and his work. It said this:

> Roberts' first wife, Carol, died of cancer in 1999. They had been married 20 years. For about a month after her death, he couldn't paint.
>
> "It was an unimaginable challenge," he says of her death. "Nobody asks to get stripped so naked as you are when you're with someone you love who's dying."
>
> He found healing in helping a group of visually impaired kids from Lincoln School paint and decorate a 6-foot-long fish for the "Something Fishy" project that placed fish sculptures all over town.
>
> "It was amazing," Roberts says. "Their noses were touching the fish as they painted. They were close

to everything. Close to the fish, close to each other, close to me. They held onto each other, like they were holding hands through a dark forest." (*The Grand Rapids Press*, October 1, 2006)

I called David's teacher later that day. She remembered everything about the project, including David's love for the process and how attached he had become to Reb.

Twenty months after losing our son, we were given a wonderful gift — stories told to us by a friend of David's we'd never known about. We also gained a new friend.

On December 14, 2006, we remembered David's birthday by again hosting an open house, this time celebrating the debut of "Alice" in our home.

Redefining

Even before he became ill, David demanded a great deal of my time and energy. In a way, my life was defined by providing his care, and I was satisfied with that role. I embraced it. Being "David's mom" was a large part of my identity and a major source of my life's focus and purpose. So, added to my grief, I now faced the future without the role and identity he provided me.

This has left me with a huge void. I meander and wander, trying to fill the emptiness and find a new role — and I have seen some success. His absence is no longer shocking to me. But often the change remains overwhelming.

Celebrating

At Christmastime 2006 Rachel and John became engaged, and a flurry of activity followed. After looking at wedding dresses with Rachel in several places, I recalled a newspaper article about a new bridal shop north of our home. Off we went to explore. The first dress Rachel tried on was a definite possibility. When she tried a second dress, we both knew instantly that it was the one.

As my daughter stood there in the dress, looking so lovely, I glanced through the large windows behind her and saw a bench, the very bench where David and I had spent so many hours listening to the Rogue River in the summer of 2004. Glimpses of grace come when least expected.

Just weeks before Rachel and John's wedding we observed David's twenty-fifth birthday at home with a few friends who gathered to eat pineapple pizza with us.

So soon, it still seemed, after burying a beloved son, Harry and I were determined to celebrate joyously the wedding of our daughter shortly after Christmas 2007. A few months later we, along with many family members, gathered to witness Jared receiving his medical degree. Before long Rachel would complete her graduate degree in speech-language pathology. Experiencing the depths of loss and despair has defined more clearly for us what is worthy of great celebration.

Our family bond, though threatened by change and loss, has strengthened through renewal and love. As we continue to live with loss and change, how grateful I am to God that we had David to teach us about love, the value of life, and the beauty of relationships.

Life continues — even joy comes — and David's spirit remains.

I still have three children.